CW01189056

The Underground Railroad

An Enthralling Overview of the Secret Path to Freedom for African Americans during the 19th Century

© Copyright 2024 - All rights reserved.

The content contained within this book may not be reproduced, duplicated, or transmitted without direct written permission from the author or the publisher.

Under no circumstances will any blame or legal responsibility be held against the publisher, or author, for any damages, reparation, or monetary loss due to the information contained within this book, either directly or indirectly.

Legal Notice:

This book is copyright protected. It is only for personal use. You cannot amend, distribute, sell, use, quote, or paraphrase any part, or the content within this book, without the consent of the author or publisher.

Disclaimer Notice:

Please note the information contained within this document is for educational and entertainment purposes only. All effort has been executed to present accurate, up-to-date, reliable, and complete information. No warranties of any kind are declared or implied. Readers acknowledge that the author is not engaging in the rendering of legal, financial, medical, or professional advice. The content within this book has been derived from various sources. Please consult a licensed professional before attempting any techniques outlined in this book.

By reading this document, the reader agrees that under no circumstances is the author responsible for any losses, direct or indirect, that are incurred as a result of the use of the information contained within this document, including, but not limited to, errors, omissions, or inaccuracies.

Free limited time bonus

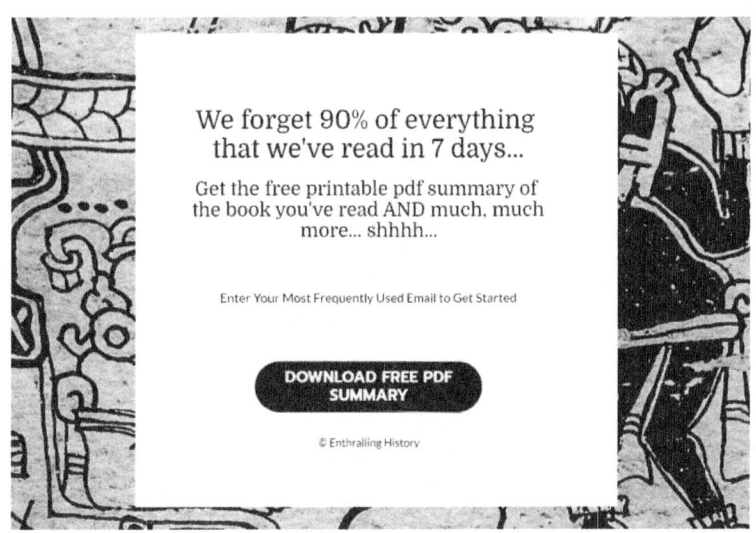

We forget 90% of everything that we've read in 7 days...

Get the free printable pdf summary of the book you've read AND much, much more... shhhh...

Enter Your Most Frequently Used Email to Get Started

DOWNLOAD FREE PDF SUMMARY

© Enthralling History

Stop for a moment. We have a free bonus set up for you. The problem is this: we forget 90% of everything that we read after 7 days. Crazy fact, right? Here's the solution: we've created a printable, 1-page pdf summary for this book that you're reading now. All you have to do to get your free pdf summary is to go to the following website: https://livetolearn.lpages.co/enthrallinghistory/

Or, Scan the QR code!

Once you do, it will be intuitive. Enjoy, and thank you!

Table of Contents

INTRODUCTION 1
CHAPTER 1: ORIGINS OF THE UNDERGROUND RAILROAD 4
CHAPTER 2: UNSUNG HEROES OF THE UNDERGROUND RAILROAD 17
CHAPTER 3: THE ROLE OF SAFE HOUSES AND SECRET CODES 34
CHAPTER 4: STORIES OF GREAT BRAVERY 42
CHAPTER 5: THE FUGITIVE SLAVE ACT AND ITS IMPACT 55
CHAPTER 6: RELIGION AND THE UNDERGROUND RAILROAD 62
CHAPTER 7: THE IMPACT OF THE UNDERGROUND RAILROAD ON AFRICAN AMERICAN LIFE 67
CHAPTER 8: INFLUENCES ON AMERICAN LITERATURE AND ART 75
CHAPTER 9: THE ROLE OF WOMEN 82
CHAPTER 10: THE LEGACY OF THE UNDERGROUND RAILROAD 92
CONCLUSION 95
HERE'S ANOTHER BOOK BY ENTHRALLING HISTORY THAT YOU MIGHT LIKE 98
FREE LIMITED TIME BONUS 99
BIBLIOGRAPHY 100

Introduction

If you grew up in the United States of America, you've undoubtedly learned about the Underground Railroad during your years in school. Many of us have done reports on famous people related to the Underground Railroad, like Harriet Tubman or Fredrick Douglass.

What if I told you that some of the information you've learned in school may be incorrect? There are a significant number of myths related to the history of the Underground Railroad that are continually perpetuated in American schools.

See if any of these statements sound familiar to you:

The Underground Railroad was run by abolitionists, most of whom were white Quakers.

The Underground Railroad was spread throughout the Southern US.

Many of the escaping enslaved people moved from safe house to safe house, hiding in secret rooms along the way.

Quilts were created and sewn by enslaved people and hung in windows to alert people on the run to the location of safe homes.

Entire families were able to escape their enslavers and travel along the Underground Railroad north to freedom together as one unit.

Were you taught these facts in class? As it turns out, these are common myths about the Underground Railroad.

This book aims to share the facts of the true Underground Railroad, dispelling these myths and replacing them with the truth. You will gain a better understanding of the treacherous journeys undertaken by enslaved people as they fled to freedom and be given thinking points to inspire further research about the brave men and women who participated in the Underground Railroad and helped create its vital role in United States history.

In the following chapters, you will find information about how the Underground Railroad began, stories of the quiet heroes who are lesser known, facts about the most famous abolitionists, the nitty-gritty details about the Fugitive Slave Act, and the role of women along the Underground Railroad.

Before we continue, however, please take a moment to consider the terms used in this book.

In the past, historical books about the Underground Railroad used the terms slave, master, and owner. Many of us grew up with these same terms when we learned United States history in school.

While these are not necessarily inappropriate words to use, thoughtful consideration has gone into the way the terms portray Black people and their struggle for freedom and equality.

Referring to African Americans as "slaves" reduces their existence to simply that—nothing but slaves. It gives a narrowly defined status. In this book, we want to share the reality of who these people were. They were mothers, fathers, brothers, and sisters. They had hopes and dreams. They went to work; they came home and rested. They felt pain; they longed for freedom. They were fully human and far more than just slaves or someone's property.

When you instead read the words "enslaved person," you're given a whole picture. This is a human being who happens to be enslaved. The person who is enslaved should first be considered a human, and only second to that should we consider their status or struggles.

When meeting a person out in public you might ask them, "Who are you?" They would give you their name first, and later you might find out where they work. You would never walk up to someone you barely know, or someone with whom you share mutual respect, and ask them, "What are you?"

The same thought process goes for the terms "slaveholder" or "enslaver." To refer to them as "masters" or "slave owners" implies that one can own a human being. Instead, they legally held the person as a slave, or they enslaved them.

The Underground Railroad was not a physical train track. It had no train station and no train cars. However, in the pages following, you will meet the brave conductors on this invisible railroad.

The famous abolitionist Frederick Douglass said, "Life and liberty are the most sacred of all man's rights."[1] This is perhaps the most eloquent statement from an abolitionist that sums up what inspired so many people to fight for their freedom and the freedom of their fellow human beings.

---

[1] Foner, Philip S., editor Taylor, Yuval *Frederick Douglass, Frederick Douglass: Selected Speeches and Writings*, editor. (Chicago: Lawrence Hill Books, 1975),180.

Chapter 1: Origins of the Underground Railroad

There is no distinct date the Underground Railroad began. Instead, the murky origins of the Underground Railroad can be glimpsed throughout the late eighteenth century and early nineteenth centuries by searching for historical clues, namely in the form of a mention here and there in quotes, speeches, or letters. These brief mentions are usually of escape routes facilitated by abolitionists, Quakers, or free Black people. Or, you might find a line written in a letter from an enslaver who had a person run away from their farm.

 The first of these quiet clues can be seen in a complaint written down by George Washington in 1786 when he was upset that religious Quakers had attempted to liberate one of his neighbor's enslaved men.[2]

 Thirty years later, a Quaker man named Isaac T. Hopper began arranging an escape network in the city of Philadelphia designed to help enslaved people run away from captivity. It didn't yet have an official title, but it was one of several early routes that began to bring together what would one day be known as the famous Underground Railroad.

Abolitionists

To better understand the different roles played by people along the Underground Railroad, it's important to understand what an abolitionist

---

[2] "Underground Railroad." Quakers in the world.

is and how they were vital to the network of safe houses along the secret routes that made up the Underground Railroad. Abolitionists are people who fight for the complete elimination, or abolition, of a specific unjust practice. In the case of nineteenth-century abolitionists, they fought for a complete end to the enslavement of Black people in the United States.

Abolitionists were opposed to slavery on every front. It was against their moral code, for personal or religious reasons. They argued that every human being had a natural right to be free; therefore, slavery was a violation of human rights.

They worked fervently to bring an end to the social acceptance of slavery. The abolitionists also fought to change the laws that allowed white men to own Black human beings. They called for the emancipation of all enslaved people immediately.

Anti-slavery societies were formed to spread information and educate people. In the days before the internet, cell phones, and email, it was necessary to spread the word through pamphlets, leaflets, and secret meetings. The anti-slavery societies used these methods to gain new followers and grow their movement. They sent people to lobby Congress, ran for political offices, and blasted anti-slavery literature throughout the Southern United States.

They also spoke out publicly with speeches and published writings. This took some courage, as the rich men who owned enslaved people were not eager to allow anyone to speak out against their comfortable way of life. Abolitionists faced backlash from their friends, family, and neighbors, and sometimes even found themselves the subjects of mob violence or arrest.

Civil disobedience is the terminology for the method abolitionists used to encourage changes in the legal system and social acceptance of emancipation for enslaved people. Civil disobedience by abolitionists included refusing to comply with laws supporting slavery. Ultimately, the boldest act of civil disobedience led to participating in the Underground Railroad, which meant helping enslaved people escape the South and travel north to freedom.

Every abolitionist faced a moral dilemma. Was noncompliance with slave laws acceptable if slavery was considered immoral? Which is worse: not following the laws of your country, or following a law that brings serious harm to another human being? The answer to this dilemma led many people, both Black and white, to join forces and facilitate the Underground Railroad. For abolitionists, it was far worse to follow laws that brought harm to others.

Since the first enslaved people set foot on the North American continent in the early 1600s, there have been those who opposed the institution of slavery. Notably, in 1816, the American Colonization Society decided a compromise between abolitionists and slavery supporters would be to free slaves and return them to somewhere in Africa. This idea was designed to end the institution of slavery without releasing thousands of Black people into the United States population.

By the year 1860, twelve thousand Black people had been returned to Africa.[3] This was known as the back-to-Africa movement.[4] It seems the African American people weren't consulted in this plan. Instead, it was assumed by Europeans and white slaveholders in the United States that enslaved peoples would want to return to Africa.

This plan presented a multitude of issues, the least of which was that Africa is not a small, homogenous country. Africa is an entire continent filled with thousands of villages, tribes, and diverse people groups. The enslaved people who were brought from Africa against their will came from multiple areas of this large continent.

The second issue that presented itself might be an obvious one. In some cases, several generations had passed since the family of an enslaved person had been in Africa. These people had lost their language and cultural identity and could no longer survive in the harsh African climates from which their ancestors had come.

On a related note, the back-to-Africa movement had no understanding or consideration of biological resistance to disease. The African Americans who traveled back to Africa often died of illnesses to which they had no immunity.

The mortality rate of African American settlers who returned to Africa is the highest among any settlers in recorded human history. For example, 4,571 arrived in the African country of Liberia between 1820 and 1843. Of those 4,571 people, only 1,819 survived. About 60 percent of the settlers died.

---

[3] "Abolitionist Movement - Definition & Famous Abolitionists | HISTORY"

[4] "Back-to-Africa movement."

For many Black and African American people, going back to an African colony was not part of their hopes and dreams. Instead, they wished to remain in the Americas, where many of them had been born. They simply longed to be free and allowed to live in the same way a white person lived—in their own home, with a job that paid a fair wage.

For some, the Underground Railroad was a viable option to reach freedom. These brave individuals often traveled alone, but they were inspired by famous Black abolitionists such as Harriet Tubman, Frederick Douglass, William Still, William Wells Brown, Sojourner Truth, and Henry Highland Garnet. You'll hear more about most of these men and women, along with a few lesser-known abolitionists, in later chapters of this book.

The Timeline of the History of Slavery in the United States

Before we dive into the stories and struggles of the brave men and women who contributed to the Underground Railroad, it's important to have a good grasp of the history of slavery in the United States. This will give you a mental picture of the way slavery began and ended across the country and the factors that contributed to its rise and fall.

The precursor to slavery in the United States was the Portuguese slave trade that began in the fifteenth century. Once the colonies were established in North America, South America, and the West Indies, an economy based on large plantations began to flourish. This drove the need for more enslaved people—cheap labor in mass quantities to run these big farms. Between the 1600s and the 1800s, more than twelve million Africans were kidnapped and forcibly transported to the Americas by boat.

As the scale of the slave trade spread and grew, and the plantation owners in turn became wealthier, so did people's knowledge of the brutality of slavery. More people came to understand how enslaved persons were suffering, and this led to emotional reactions from people throughout the colonies and early United States. From there, abolitionists were spurred to action.

To view the history of slavery in the United States is to see the slow unfolding of an institution of barbarity, as the slave trade fueled rich landowners' rise to wealth and power. Alongside this barbarity, we can also view the unfolding of hope and witness the power of the common man to fight back against what he feels is morally unacceptable. As you read through the timeline below, look for these two common threads intertwining across more than two hundred years of history.

Each year on this timeline is marked by an important event in history, whether a person's experience, a struggle between slaveholders and enslaved people, or a law that was passed.

1619

This was the year the first African people were brought onto North American soil. They were likely taken from a Portuguese slave ship and arrived in a group of around twenty Africans. They sailed into Jamestown, Virginia, where they were promptly traded for goods. However, they were not named slaves at this point. They were classified as indentured servants.

1640

Three indentured servants ran away and were captured. Two of the servants were white. The third was a Black man named John Punch. The white men were assigned to serve more years as indentured servants as punishment. But John Punch? He was sentenced to be an indentured servant for life, making him the first enslaved person, the first enslaved person in Virginia and in what would become the United States.

1641

Massachusetts legalized slavery, becoming the first of the colonies to recognize enslaving human beings as a practice in early United States history.

1662

A law in Virginia was passed stating that if the mother was a slave, the child would also be a slave regardless of who the father was. This was the first step toward developing the Virginia Slave Codes that would be implemented in 1705.

1676

Both white and Black people in Virginia united to fight under Nathaniel Bacon against the wealthy elite landowners and the governor of Virginia in Bacon's Rebellion. Though the rebellion fizzled out when Bacon suddenly died of illness, it served as an important wake-up call for the wealthy. Realizing they could be outnumbered, they began rushing to create stricter laws regarding slavery and stronger class distinctions that would empower the wealthy and keep the poor weak and separated from each other.

1688

On February 16, 1688, the Quakers in Pennsylvania stood together in unison as they drafted their own anti-slavery resolution. It was the first anti-slavery resolution for any group in the history of the early United States.

1705

In a significant historical move, the Virginia Slave Code codified the status of enslaved people in the state. To codify laws means to gather all the laws and statutes together, organize them, and make them clear and accessible so they are easily recognized and enforced. For Virginian African Americans, this further limited their freedoms, defining the rights enslavers were granted over them. Notably, the Virginia Slave Code allowed enslavers to punish their enslaved without any fear of legal repercussions. It also laid out specific rewards for the capture of runaway enslaved people.

1712

In New York City at this time, the population was around six thousand to eight thousand people. One thousand of those people were enslaved. The colonial governor of New York, Robert Hunter, wrote about the beginning of the rebellion. He said, "One ... slave to one Vantilburgh set fire to [a shed] of his masters, and then repairing to his place where the rest were, they all sallied out together with their arms and marched to the fire. By this time, the noise of the fire spreading through the town, the people began to flock to it. Upon the approach of several, the slaves fired and killed them."[5]

During the battle to regain control, nine of the white enslavers were killed. Six others suffered serious injuries. As the Black people fled, the local militia was awakened, and soldiers were immediately sent out to capture them. They located twenty-seven people hiding in the nearby swamp.

Six of the men committed suicide rather than face trial. Most of the others were convicted and faced terrible, brutal public executions, including being burned alive or hung by chains in the center of the city

---

[5] Lewis, Danny : "The New York Slave Revolt of 1712 Was a Bloody Prelude to Decades of Hardship | Smart News| Smithsonian Magazine."

for all to witness.

This battle marked a significant turn in the lives of enslaved people living in New York. The city strengthened its laws against Black people, no longer allowing them to own firearms or even gather in large groups. Enslavers were now allowed to beat African Americans as much as they desired, as long as the people weren't permanently maimed.

To discourage enslavers from freeing their enslaved, they were required to first post a $200 bond. That was a large sum of money at the time. New York would outlaw slavery in 1799, as abolitionists gained momentum in the area. However, the region continued to profit from products created by enslaved people in the Caribbean, such as molasses and sugar, through the time of the Civil War.

1770

We have arrived at the beginning of the American Revolution. A Black man was one of the first people killed in the opening days of the Revolutionary War.

Crispus Attucks was shot in the chest by two musket balls fired from a British rifle on March 5, 1770. Four other men were killed alongside him. This became known as the Boston Massacre.

Crispus Attucks was a man of mixed ancestry. He was partially African American and partially Native American. The surname Attucks is of indigenous origin. It comes from the Natick tribe's word for deer. His name was originally given as Michael Johnson, which was either the Christianized name given to him by his enslavers or an alias he adopted to protect himself from being recaptured after his escape. Historians have noted an advertisement for an escaped enslaved person named "Crispas" in the *Boston Gazette*. He is listed as being born in Framingham, Massachusetts. At the time of his death, Attucks was living in New Providence, Bahamas as a sailor.

The attack and subsequent death of Attucks happened when he and a group of other sailors gathered to march along King Street in Boston, brandishing clubs and ice balls to swing and throw at the British soldiers. Chaos ensued, and the soldiers fired their muskets into the crowd, killing Attucks and the four other men.

The attack occurred as tensions rose between British soldiers and laborers. The British often took part-time jobs away from laborers by accepting the work for lower wages.

The famous John Adams, who was at the time a lawyer for the British Crown, portrayed the attack as being started by "a motley rabble of saucy boys, Negroes, and mulattos, Irish teagues and outlandish jack tars."[6] This language was meant to demean the attackers by calling them lower-class people who were Black or Irish and sailors not local to the area.

The British soldiers and their commanding officer were acquitted at trial, and this further contributed to a growing public fury against the British soldiers occupying Boston.

1775

On April 14 of this year, the Pennsylvania Abolition Society was founded, signaling a growing number of citizens in the northern region were dissatisfied with the institution of slavery and working to bring about changes.

As the battle for independence grew to a full-scale war in 1775, around five thousand African American men served in the fight as soldiers and sailors. They were both free Black men and enslaved people. Surprisingly, they were given nearly equal treatment to white soldiers, except for being barred from holding higher ranks.

1776

On July 4, 1776, the Continental Congress adopted the Declaration of Independence, marking the end of the Revolutionary War and the beginning of the United States as a country independent from Great Britain.

1793

On February 12, 1793, Congress passed the first Fugitive Slave Act. This made it illegal to harbor a runaway enslaved person or interfere with a runaway slave being arrested.

1800

The first major slave rebellion was planned near Richmond, Virginia, under the pretense of a religious meeting. However, a thunderstorm delayed events, and two members betrayed the enslaved people who had planned to participate. Up to one thousand slaves had planned to participate in the rebellion.

---

[6] Kidder, Adams, Weems, *History of the Boston Massacre, March 5, 1770 : consisting of the narrative of the town, the trial of the soldiers and a historical introduction, containing unpublished* (Albany: J. Munsell, 1870), 255.

1816

This was the year the American Colonization Society was founded to transport freed Black people back to Africa. An African colony was created. It would become the Republic of Liberia in 1847.

1831

Nat Turner led the most well-known and brutal slave rebellion in the history of the United States, involving around seventy-five Black men. They killed sixty white people. The rebellion lasted two days, August 21 and 22. On the 21st, Turner and his band of men carried out their attacks. On the 22nd, white men took their revenge, killing three dozen Black men without trial and regaining control of the region.

Southern communities feared further revolts. For some, this encouraged emancipation, as people were beginning to see that the institution of slavery might not be a viable way of life.

1839

A slave revolt occurred on a slave ship called *La Amistad*. This caused a political debate, ending in a hallmark decision by the United States Supreme Court declaring the captive people aboard *La Amistad* as free. They had the right to resist being unlawfully enslaved.

1850

The Fugitive Slave Act of 1850 was a blow for enslaved people and abolitionists working toward freedom. This act required that escaped enslaved people be sent back to their owners, no matter where they were captured. This meant that people who escaped north to states where slavery had been outlawed were no longer safe. They could be hunted down and returned to the South, facing harsh punishments.

The act gave the responsibility for finding and returning escaped people to the federal government, which gave power to the US Marshals Service and other federal men across the entire United States, organizing the return of enslaved people to their enslavers as never before.

The Fugitive Slave Act of 1850 made the Canadian border the end goal for all people traveling the Underground Railroad, as this was the only place they could now truly be safe and live as free human beings.

1852

This year, the famous book *Uncle Tom's Cabin*, a powerful anti-slavery novel, was published. However, dramatizations based on the book were performed all over the United States, which portrayed harmful characterizations of Black people and led to the spread of common stereotypes that would persist well after the end of slavery in the United States.

1854

The Kansas-Nebraska Act was a new mandate that stated settlers in new United States territories would decide if these regions became free or slave states. At this point, the Republican Party, which had been recently formed, gained strength and vowed to prevent new states from becoming slave states. The Republican Party quickly became the leading party in almost all the northern states and territories, a victory for the enslaved people and the abolitionists working to free them.

1857

In another hallmark case called *Dred Scott v. Sanford*, the United States Supreme Court passed a ruling stating that Black people were not official citizens of the United States. This case also led to Congress being unable to prohibit slavery in any state or territory.

Dred Scott was a free Black man who had been born as an enslaved person in Missouri and moved by his enslaver to Illinois, leaving him residing in a state where slavery had been outlawed. He tried to purchase his freedom in the free state, and he was denied, leading to the trial. The Supreme Court decision meant that he was not entitled to his freedom simply because he resided in a free state.

In a divisive move, the case also rolled back part of the Missouri Compromise, which had declared the territories west of Missouri and north of latitude 36°30′ as free, declaring it was unconstitutional.

1860 to 1861

At this point in history, Abraham Lincoln was elected as president. Rising tensions between slave states and free states came to a head, leaving the slave states in the South to secede from the Union.

At the start of the Civil War in 1860, the population of Black people according to the census was 4,441,830. Of those people, 3,953,760 were enslaved and 488,070 were free. Around 185,000 soldiers fought for the Union and their freedom.

The 54th Massachusetts Volunteer Infantry was the first all-Black regiment recruited from men in the North for the Union Army. Its most heroic attack was on Fort Wagner in North Carolina.

1863

On January 1, 1863, President Lincoln issued the Emancipation Proclamation. While the war still raged on in final battles, this proclamation meant that if the North won the war, slavery would end in the United States of America.

1865

Two long years later on December 6, 1865, the Thirteenth Amendment to the United States Constitution was officially ratified, bringing an end to the institution of slavery in the US.

How the Underground Railroad Got Its Name

Now that you've viewed a timeline with the basic events of the history of slavery in the United States, we can circle back to our original topic: the Underground Railroad.

The year we're focusing on now is 1842. On our timeline, this is after the famous Nat Turner revolt and before the brutal Fugitive Slave Act of 1850. At this point, the clandestine escape routes from the Southern United States into the free Northern states and on to Canada hadn't been given an official name.

At least, the routes were unnamed until Thomas Smallwood entered the scene.

Thomas Smallwood is not a well-known figure in Black history. In fact, most people today have never heard of this man. He was born in 1801, just outside of the Washington, D.C., area as an enslaved person. In 1831, he managed to buy his freedom.

Smallwood was living as a free man in 1842. He ran an innocuous shoe-making business out of his home near the nation's capital, where he lived with his wife and children. At night, Smallwood was busy coordinating and organizing dozens of journeys to freedom for enslaved people. These early routes of the Underground Railroad led out of Baltimore, away from Washington and surrounding counties.

Smallwood was what we could call a conductor on the yet-unnamed Underground Railroad. He was an outspoken abolitionist, as well.

Do you remember the common Underground Railroad myths mentioned in the introduction of this book? One of them stated, "The Underground Railroad was run by abolitionists, most of whom were white Quakers."

That is false. The Underground Railroad was mostly run by free Black people like Smallwood who lived throughout the northern states, with assistance and support from white Quakers at times.

Thomas Smallwood was also a writer. He wrote for an abolitionist newspaper published in Albany, New York.[7] Thomas's writing was brutally honest. He held back nothing in his vitriol for enslavers, and he also wrote openly of those who had managed to escape to the north. He boldly used each person's real name, except for his own. To protect himself and his family, he wrote under a pseudonym.

For many years, Thomas Smallwood's articles were lost to time, relegated to a dusty stack in a Boston Public Library warehouse. That is until *The New York Times* reporter Scott Shane stumbled upon them when doing research for a book on Thomas Smallwood.[8]

Within Smallwood's articles, Shane found the first known published use of the term "Underground Railroad."

The phrase first appeared in an article published on August 10, 1842, in the abolitionist newspaper *The Tocsin of Liberty*. Smallwood wrote with mockery and sarcasm, telling enslavers that their "walking property" had "walked off." When he began making references to the enslaved people seeming to disappear into thin air, he joked it was as if they had climbed aboard a mysterious underground railroad and were spirited away.

This sarcastic answer to how many African Americans were disappearing became a running theme in Smallwood's future articles. He told white men who were missing their workers to go apply at the "office of the underground railroad" in Washington to search for information on their missing property. He then began referring to himself as the "general agent of all branches of the National Underground Railroad."

Thanks to the dedicated research of Shane Scott, we have uncovered this hidden truth about the origins of the Underground Railroad's name. Scott goes on to say that he thoroughly researched other mentions of the Underground Railroad in publications, only to find most of them were based on folklore or myths and dated long after Smallwood's scathing abolitionist articles.

---

[7] "Opinion | How the Underground Railroad Got Its Name - The New York Times"
[8] Shane Scott *Flee North: A Forgotten Hero and the Fight for Freedom in Slavery's Borderland*

As more and more abolitionists read the phrase "Underground Railroad" in Smallwood's publications, the name began to spread like wildfire. In just a few years, the term "Underground Railroad" was being used to reference the many paths to freedom taken by enslaved people in a wide range of articles, books, and leaflets.

Thomas Smallwood's writing and tireless work to organize escape routes were both paramount in giving enslaved people the courage and the leg up they needed to begin their journeys to freedom. It's important to acknowledge that men like Smallwood are often overshadowed in history by the more well-known work of white allies who came alongside free Black people to assist them as abolitionists and conductors on the Underground Railroad.

The discovery of Smallwood's long-lost writings and his arduous work behind the scenes is a perfect example of why we need to look past the friendly, whitewashed history stories we've learned at school. Instead, we should take time to dig deeper to uncover the truth about the pain and hope that fueled the Underground Railroad along its invisible tracks northward.

Chapter 2: Unsung Heroes of the Underground Railroad

The heartbeat of the Underground Railroad was powered by the very people it existed to assist: The Black men and women who bravely made perilous journeys to freedom in the North and those who had already achieved freedom yet continued risking their lives to help end slavery.

Wilbur Siebert

Our first short biography is of a person who is historically famous. While not necessarily an unsung hero, he bears mentioning here as a significant person. First, he collected a large amount of information from people about their experiences with the Underground Railroad. Second, there is controversy today surrounding some of the information that Siebert published. Perhaps unknowingly, Siebert played an important role in perpetuating some of the myths surrounding the Underground Railroad and contributing to the whitewashing of history.

Who was Wilbur Siebert?

Wilbur Siebert was a professor of history at Ohio State University from 1891 to 1935 and Professor Emeritus from 1935 to 1961. Siebert published a famous study in 1898 called *The Underground Railroad from Slavery to Freedom.* In this study, Siebert included a collection of stories he gathered about the Underground Railroad. His method of research involved creating a survey of seven questions related to slavery and the Underground Railroad. He called this his Underground Railroad Circular, which he sent out to people who had taken part in the

Underground Railroad, or their friends and family, in 1892.

The questions on the circular were as follows:
1) What route of the Underground Railroad did you know about or follow? Give names and locations of the stations and names of the Station Keepers.
2) In what time period was the Underground Railroad active?
3) How did the Underground Railroad operate, and how did members communicate with each other?
4) Share memorable incidents, including the dates, locations, and people involved.
5) Give your personal connection and history with the Underground Railroad.
6) Share the names and addresses of any other people you know who may be willing to contribute information about the Underground Railroad.
7) Give a brief biography about yourself.

The response Siebert received from his Underground Railroad Circular was phenomenal. He was given hundreds of stories, anecdotes, and little-known details from the people who had taken his survey. The responses went on for so long that Siebert continued accepting information until 1954.

He used all these stories to write three more books about the Underground Railroad.

The Underground Railroad in Massachusetts was published in 1936. He went on to write *Vermont's Anti-Slavery and Underground Railroad Record* in 1937, and finally, he published The *Mysteries of Ohio's Underground Railroad* in 1951.[9] Today, his work is still known as the Underground Railroad's most comprehensive study.

As time passed, the Underground Railroad became a sort of tall tale in American history. Stories became fantastical or exaggerated. People were enamored with the idea of a mysterious escape route, facilitated by famous characters like Harriet Tubman.

Modern historians began to scrutinize some of the records published by Siebert as the years went on. Some of the details seemed too wild to

---

[9] "Wilbur Siebert Historian or Fabulist | World History"

be true, and while nothing can be completely proven false, it has become apparent that point of view matters when learning about history.

Siebert relied heavily on his friends and acquaintances when he gathered information, and these people were, like him, largely white males. This skewed the perspective in his publications, leaving out the first-person point of view of actual Black men and women who experienced slavery and risked their lives escaping along the Underground Railroad.

Siebert claimed that thousands of white abolitionists helped the fugitive enslaved people along their escape route north. This claim has been somewhat debunked by historians in the present. It is unlikely that enslaved people would automatically trust a white person, who could return them to their enslavers at any moment, not to mention that it was illegal for a white person to help anyone who was trying to escape slavery! In the South, a person aiding an escapee would get jail time and face violence from their friends and neighbors. The constitutionally protected right to free speech was boldly suppressed in 1836 when an order was given prohibiting abolitionists from being heard or their petitions from being read at the Supreme Court. Even in the North, abolitionists faced being ostracized by their communities, making it unlikely that there was a large underground community of white people who were in a hurry to help Black freedom seekers.

When reading historical information about marginalized people like those who traveled the Underground Railroad, it's always important to carefully consider the bias and point of view of your sources, including whether they are primary sources with firsthand accounts or secondary sources that are retellings by other people.

History is often told by the victors or repeated from the point of view of the loudest person in the room. Seeking out the stories of the underdogs and the unsung heroes will give us a more accurate and well-rounded version of what people experienced.

What remains is the need for modern historians to carefully study the information and accounts Siebert collected and published from an objective point of view to determine what is truth and what amounts to sentimental recollections or hazy memories.

William Still

William Still.
https://commons.wikimedia.org/wiki/File:William_Still_abolitionist.jpg

One of the most important historical narratives we have about the Underground Railroad was written by William Still. Published in 1872 and simply titled *The Underground Railroad*, this book gives many first-person accounts of enslaved people's experiences in slavery and the perilous travels they undertook to make it north to freedom, including near-death escapes.

The book contains firsthand accounts from 649 enslaved people who risked their lives escaping to freedom, along with information and stories from conductors of the Underground Railroad and famous abolitionists. William Still also included his collection of ransom notes, letters, and memos to go alongside the stories.

Because of his first-person sources, William Still's book is considered far more historically accurate than the better-known book by Wilbur Siebert.

Who was William Still, aside from an author?

Still was born on October 7, 1821, in Burlington County, New Jersey as a free person. He was the baby of his family, the youngest of eighteen siblings. His father, Levin Still, had purchased his freedom years prior, and his mother, Charity Still, had escaped slavery in Maryland to the free state of New Jersey.

Still's parents raised him to be well aware of the horrors of slavery in the South. They raised their children to take pride in their hard work and taught them to remain determined to succeed even when facing adversity.

As an adult, William Still married Letitia George and moved to Philadelphia. They had four children together. Still was hired by the Pennsylvania Society for the Abolition of Slavery, where he became a clerk. He was the first Black man permitted to join the society and the first Black man to hold this important job. It was at this point his involvement in the Underground Railroad took off. He became active in the Underground Railroad, assisting fugitives on the run as they arrived in Philadelphia for twenty years before the Civil War.

After the Fugitive Slave Act passed in 1850, the city's vigilance committee was revived. The committee served to help freedom seekers on their journey, and they appointed William Still as the chairman.

William Still's first major life accomplishment was teaching himself to read and write. At this time, simply learning basic phonics and grammar was seen as an act of rebellion for African Americans. It was illegal for a Black person to learn to read and write, in an attempt to keep them ignorant and enslaved.

Learning to read and write gave William Still an advantage in life. He began keeping business records, and most importantly, he started to collect artifacts and firsthand accounts from the enslaved people he met as a conductor on the Underground Railroad.

He wrote a letter to the press in 1859 to publicize the discrimination African Americans faced when riding the streetcars in Philadelphia. He later went on to publish a twenty-eight-page address on the same subject titled *A Brief Narrative of the Struggle for the Rights of the Colored People of Philadelphia in the City Railway Cars.*[10] On April 8, 1867, his address was read before a large public audience at Liberty Hall on Lombard Street in Philadelphia.

William Still continued fighting for the equality of the Black man through continual research, writing, and participating in activism even after the Civil War, until his death in 1902.

---

[10] William Still: An African American Abolitionist

Josiah Henson

Josiah Henson.
https://commons.wikimedia.org/wiki/File:Josiah_Henson_bw.jpg

Josiah Henson was born as an enslaved person in 1789. He grew up in Maryland and was sold away from his father and five siblings to a new enslaver in Kentucky. He describes the pain and sorrow of being forcibly removed from his family in his book, *The Life of Josiah Henson: Formerly a Slave, Now an Inhabitant of Canada, as Narrated by Himself.*

Henson became a Methodist preacher while enslaved in Kentucky. He married a woman named Charlotte and had four children with her. In September of 1830, things in Henson's life came to a head, as he attempted to purchase his freedom and failed. Fearing he would be sold away from his family into the Deep South of New Orleans, Henson instead decided to make the courageous decision to flee the South with his family.

He took his wife and children, and they escaped across the Ohio River into Indiana. From there, they made it further north to Canada. Henson noted the date his family crossed the Canadian border into freedom. It was October 28, 1830.

Once in Canada, Henson became an abolitionist. He set in motion plans to do everything he could to help enslaved people back in the United States. Henson founded the Dawn Settlement. This was a place meant to house Black settlers who had recently arrived in Canada after fleeing slavery. To assist these people in starting new lives, the Dawn Settlement taught them valuable trades so that they could have a career in their new homeland.

In his narrative, Josiah wrote about making multiple trips back over the border into the United States, where he visited with many famous authors and abolitionists.

Henry Wadsworth Longfellow mentions giving money for the cause to Henson many times over the years. He also describes a visit by Henson to his home in Cambridge, Massachusetts, writing the following in a journal entry from 1846, "In the evening Mr. Henson, a Negro, once a slave, now a preacher, called to get subscription for the school at Dawn, in Upper Canada, for education of blacks. I had a long talk with him, and he gave me an account of his escape from slavery with his family."[11]

It's also said that Harriet Beecher Stowe based her character Uncle Tom, from the book *Uncle Tom's Cabin*, on Josiah Henson.

He assisted hundreds of people in both reaching freedom and starting successful new lives after their escape. Henson lived long enough to witness the Civil War and to see the end of slavery in the United States. He died in Dresden, Ontario, Canada, in 1883.

Rev. Leonard Grimes

Leonard Andrew Grimes.
https://commons.wikimedia.org/wiki/File:REV._LEONARD_ANDREW_GRIMES.JPG

---

[11] Josiah Henson (U.S. National Park Service)

Leonard Grimes was born in Leesburg, Virginia, in 1815. His parents were free African Americans. Grimes took a trip through the Southern United States, where he was utterly horrified at the reality of slavery for Black Americans. It was after this trip that Grimes became an abolitionist. He vowed to do everything in his power to assist enslaved people on their journeys to freedom.

In the 1830s, Grimes started a coach business in the District of Columbia. He quickly discovered this was an excellent way to participate in the growing Underground Railroad. After helping hundreds of freedom seekers on their escape routes, Grimes was arrested and convicted in 1839. He was sentenced to two years of hard labor at the Richmond Penitentiary. Before he was released, he had to pay a fine of $100, which was a significant amount of money for the time.

After this, Grimes left the District of Columbia with his family and moved to New Bedford, Massachusetts, before eventually settling in Boston. There, Grimes became a Baptist minister at the Twelfth Baptist Church. Working with his church, which had many formerly enslaved people among the members, Grimes worked to provide funds to freedom seekers and those who found themselves in court for the crime of escaping slavery.

Grimes and his congregation became known as "The Fugitive Slave Church." They rallied the Boston Black and abolitionist community to become involved in every case of a fugitive slave that went to court. They participated in the infamous case of Anthony Burns, raising money to travel to Baltimore, where they raised more funds to purchase Anthony Burns's freedom.

"Much of what we call the Underground Railroad was actually operated clandestinely by African Americans themselves through urban vigilance committees and rescue squads that were often led by free blacks," said David Blight in his book *Passages to Freedom: The Underground Railroad in History and Memory.*[12]

Leonard Grimes was a perfect example of this.

Grimes also helped fight for the creation of a Black regiment to fight in the Civil War. His actions helped result in the founding of the 54th Massachusetts Infantry Regiment in 1863, which was one of the first and

---

[12] Gates Jr, Louis Henry Myths About the Underground Railroad | African American History Blog | The African Americans: Many Rivers to Cross

most prominent infantry regiments made up of Black men.

Leonard Grimes died in 1873, having spent most of his life as a proud abolitionist and conductor on the Underground Railroad, assisting many of his fellow Black brothers and sisters on their quest to reach safety and freedom in Canada.

Lewis Hayden

Lewis Hayden.
https://commons.wikimedia.org/wiki/File:Lewis_Hayden_Portrait.png

Lewis Hayden was born as an enslaved person in Kentucky. He married Esther Harvey, who was sold, along with their child, to the famous Kentucky senator Henry Clay. She was then sold again to someone else, and Lewis never saw his wife or child again.

In 1842, Hayden married a second time to a woman named Harriet Hayden. A few years later, the couple escaped and traveled north to freedom, along with their son Joseph. They first went to Detroit and then on to Canada. They had a daughter named Elizabeth, and together they decided to return as a family to the United States to fight for the freedom of other enslaved African Americans. They settled in Boston, Massachusetts, and opened a successful clothing store.

Lewis Hayden went on to become an influential figure as part of Boston's Black community on Beacon Hill, as well as a prominent abolitionist. Hayden was a part of the Boston Vigilance Committee, serving as part of the insular executive committee. The goal of the vigilance committee was to prevent fugitive enslaved people from being captured and returned to slavery.

Hayden used his own home as a meeting place for abolitionists, a safe house for enslaved people following the Underground Railroad north, and a place to facilitate further transportation for those who were traveling. He also collected donated clothing and funds to assist people on their journey north out of Boston.

He had several notable run-ins with the law. At one point, he and his wife Harriet provided a safe haven for William and Ellen Craft. They had escaped slavery in Georgia a few years prior and had happily settled in Boston as boarders in the Haydens' home—until the Fugitive Slave Law allowed slave catchers into the free state of Massachusetts to pursue them. Warrants were put out for their arrest in an attempt to force the couple to return to slavery in the South.

The Haydens barricaded the doorway of their home, threatening the slave catchers who were chasing after the Crafts, refusing to let them be taken. Craft and Hayden let the US Marshals know they had a keg of gunpowder under the house and were ready to light the fuse at any moment should the slave catchers breach the doorway. Their resolve and threats were so strong that the US Marshals called off the hunt for William and Ellen Craft. The Crafts later escaped to England.

The Haydens' home is now a national historic site at 66 Phillips (formerly Southac) Street in Boston.[13]

Lewis Hayden also participated in the attempts to free Shadrach Minkins, also known as Frederick Wilkins, from the Boston courthouse in 1851, which was successful. He again helped try to free Anthony Burns in 1854.

In addition to abolitionist activities, Hayden worked with other prominent leaders in the community toward equality and freedom for Black people. He fought to integrate the Boston Public Schools, working alongside William Cooper Nell.

He became the messenger to the secretary of state in the 1850s. This was an important position, one that was politically appointed and made Lewis Hayden one of the first Black employees for the state of

---

[13] Lewis and Harriet Hayden House - Boston African American National Historic Site (U.S. National Park Service)

Massachusetts. This position gave Hayden the ability to get close to and speak to many high-profile leaders, which was essential to furthering the abolitionist agenda by educating and even pressuring leaders to pass laws that supported equality and integration. Hayden was the messenger to the Massachusetts secretary of state for thirty years.

Hayden proudly recruited Black men for the Massachusetts 54th Infantry Regiment during the Civil War. Once the Civil War came to an end, he continued his work. He joined the Massachusetts General Court, serving as one of the first Black members. This was an elected position as a representative in the Massachusetts state legislature.

The inspirational and influential Lewis Hayden didn't stop there, however. He continued to be an advocate for the underdog, involving himself in the fight for equality alongside women in the suffragette movement, working toward women's right to vote. When asked why he chose to be a part of the fight for women's suffrage, he referenced the support the abolitionists received from women and said, "My race can never repay the debt we owe to such as these [suffragists]. I should be indeed an ingrate, if I did not work and vote for the enfranchisement of women."[14]

Henry Brown

Henry Box Brown.
https://commons.wikimedia.org/wiki/File:Henry_Box_Brown_(cropped).jpg

---

[14] 1873 House Bill 0122. Resolve Providing For An Amendment Of The Constitution To Secure The Elective Franchise And The Right To Hold Office To Women, Massachusetts State Library, https://archives.lib.state.ma.us/handle/2452/742347;

"Lewis Hayden Obituary," *The Woman's Journal* (Apr 13, 1889), Schlesinger Library, Radcliffe Institute, Harvard University, https://iiif.lib.harvard.edu/manifests/view/drs:49020444$123i.

Also known as Henry "Box" Brown, Henry Brown is famous for asking a shopkeeper to help him get to freedom by traveling in a shipping crate as if he were a package of goods.

Brown was born in 1815 in Virginia as an enslaved person. We don't know many details about his early life. At age fifteen, he was sent to Richmond, Virginia, to work in a tobacco factory. He got married and had four children, but to his great sorrow, his wife and children were sold further south in North Carolina. After his family was sold away from him, Brown became determined to leave the South and escape to freedom.

He worked with a fellow church member, James Caesar Anthony Smith, to come up with the daring plan. They decided Brown could seal himself inside a wooden crate that was only three feet and one inch long, two feet and six inches high, and two feet wide. The crate had three holes drilled for air. Brown decided that, to be safe, he would carry a tool to poke more air holes as he traveled in the shipping crate. He also carried water to drink.

With the help of a white acquaintance named Samuel Smith, Henry Brown was closed up in the cloth-lined crate and sent on his way. On March 23, 1849, Brown was sent from Virginia to the Pennsylvania Anti-Slavery Society in Philadelphia as a parcel. His box weighed around two hundred pounds and was labeled as "dry goods."

The journey took twenty-seven hours in total.

Along the way, the box was flipped upside down twice. At one point, Brown was trapped upside down for eighteen miles. In his narrative, he describes the experience:

"I felt my eyes swelling as if they would burst from their sockets; and the veins on my temples were dreadfully distended with pressure of blood upon my head."[15]

As Brown crawled out of his box, he recited a psalm from the Bible in thanks for his safe arrival. Shortly after arriving in Philadelphia, Brown was sent to New York City. From there, he traveled to New Bedford, Massachusetts, where he joined other abolitionists in their efforts to support enslaved people and those starting new lives in freedom.

---

[15] Brown Box, Henry *Narrative of the Life of Henry Box Brown, Written by Himself*

Brown decided to inspire others to think of creative ways to escape by traveling around New England and performing a reenactment of his experience. A publisher from Boston named Charles Stearns published a version of Henry Brown's escape. The story was so popular that it became the most well-known and retold story of an escapee in United States history.

The Fugitive Slave Act forced the well-known Brown to flee yet again, this time across the ocean to safety in England. After living there for a short time, he married again and had a child. Critics spread gossip, saying that Brown should have located his wife and four children in North Carolina and tried to purchase their freedom first.

Once it was safe, in 1875, Brown came back to the United States. He continued traveling around giving shows. However, this time he used the box from his original escape to create a magic show.

There are no details recorded about Brown's death. We only know that his last show was on February 26, 1889. Henry "Box" Brown remains one of the most popular people to escape slavery in a unique and creative way.

White Allies of the Underground Railroad

While we strive to tell the important firsthand narratives of Black free people and enslaved people who followed the Underground Railroad to freedom, some white allies also played essential roles in assisting people on their journeys north, including John Rankin, Levi Coffin, and Robert F. Wallcut. These are their stories.

Levi Coffin

Levi Coffin.
https://commons.wikimedia.org/wiki/File:Levi_coffin.JPG

Levi Coffin was born on October 28, 1798, into a Quaker family who did not believe in owning slaves. The Coffin family lived in North Carolina, where Levi saw enslaved people in his everyday life.

The Coffin family began helping runaway enslaved people by feeding them on their family farm. In 1821, William tried to open a school for enslaved people, planning to teach them to read and write, but the school failed since no enslaved person was allowed to attend.

Levi Coffin then moved to Indiana, where he helped more than 2,000 enslaved people on their way north. His home earned the nickname "Grand Central Station" due to the number of people he assisted.

In 1847, Coffin moved to Cincinnati. There, he started the Western Free Produce Association, which only sold items that were produced by free people. He also set up his new home as another stop on the Underground Railroad.

After the Civil War, Coffin raised a large sum of money for the time. He managed to gather $100,000, which he used for the Western Freedman's Aid Society, which assisted newly freed enslaved people in starting their lives.

John Rankin

John Rankin.
https://commons.wikimedia.org/wiki/File:John_Rankin_(American_abolitionist).jpg

John Rankin lived from 1793 to 1886. He was a Southern white man who became a Presbyterian minister.

Rankin moved through the South several times, eventually settling in Ripley, Ohio, where he was safer from threats. He worked tirelessly as a conductor on the Underground Railroad and fought for Black freedom his entire life.

One of his best-known stories was the time in 1838 when he assisted a woman who was crossing the Ohio River while carrying her two-year-old child. The river was partially frozen at the time, making it a little easier to pass, but nonetheless extremely terrifying. Harriet Beecher Stowe used this story to create her character Eliza Harris in the novel *Uncle Tom's Cabin*.

Angry Kentuckians knew that Rankin was helping their "property" escape to freedom. They frequently attacked his home in Ohio and even placed a $3,000 bounty on his head.

Robert F. Wallcut

Robert F. Wallcut was born in 1797. He was a Bostonian known for his activism against slavery. He was also a Unitarian minister, graduating from Harvard in 1817. He traveled throughout Massachusetts preaching.

In the 1840s, Wallcut became well-known as an abolitionist. Slavery had been abolished in Boston and Massachusetts in 1783, making the big city a hub of activity for freedom seekers on the run from their enslavers in the Southern states. Wallcut rose to the occasion, fighting for social justice. He was a member of the Massachusetts Society for the Abolition of Capital Punishment and the New England Non-Resistance Society and worked for the Massachusetts Anti-Slavery Society.

As part of the Massachusetts Anti-Slavery Society, he was the Recording Secretary for more than a decade. However, Wallcut's largest accomplishment and his biggest contribution to the anti-slavery movement was his dedication to the abolitionist publication called *The Liberator*. Wallcut wrote for *The Liberator* from 1846 to 1865.

Wallcut used *The Liberator* to help organize help for freedom seekers—enslaved people on the run, heading to freedom in the north. In *The Liberator*, Wallcut wrote that those who wished to contribute funds or clothing could send their contributions directly to him at *The Liberator*'s main office. He passed these things on to people who needed to appear well-dressed so that they blended in with society in the North and didn't appear like impoverished escapees.

Blending into the crowd was especially important for freedom seekers after the Fugitive Slave Act passed in 1850.

His call for help to the public in *The Liberator* in October 1850 read as follows:

"Alarmed at the operation of the new Fugitive Slave Law, the Fugitives from slavery are pressing Northward...They are coming to us in increasing numbers, and they look to us for aid. Oppressed by the tyranny of a heartless and God-defying government, who will help them? Their first and most earnest desire is for employment...Help us, then, all you who are friends of the fugitive, to extend to them this charity, this simple justice. Let all, who know, or can learn of places which may be filled by these men, women and youths, information by letter or otherwise, to Robert F. Wallcut, or Samuel May, Jr., 21 Cornhill, Boston...this appeal is made to you. Cannot you find, or procure, one or more places where the hunted slave may abide securely, and work through the winter? ... Many of the fugitives come very poorly provided with clothing; and those who have garments of any kind to spare, will be sure to confer them on the suffering and needy by sending them, marked 'For fugitives,' at 21 Cornhill, as above."[16]

Wallcut didn't just write for *The Liberator*. He also helped publish the paper and worked as an agent to procure other writers. He facilitated the publishing of one of the first known African American history books called *Colored Patriots of the American Revolution* by William Cooper Nells, and a second book called *The Rendition of Anthony Burns* by William I. Bowditch.

Wallcut went beyond writing. He was also an abolitionist who participated in the Boston Vigilance Committee. Today, we can look back at the records of the Boston Vigilance Committee and see that Wallcut helped forty-four freedom seekers who were named. He also assisted many people who remain unnamed, giving them things like clothing or furniture so that they could establish a life around Boston or fares to Canada as they finalized their escape plans.

Wallcut escorted the famous Harriet Beecher Stowe, author of the book *Uncle Tom's Cabin*, to meet up with thirteen freedom seekers at a safe house in 1853.

As the Civil War ended and the need for abolitionists faded away, *The Liberator* put out its final issue in December of 1865, citing Robert F. Wallcut as an "honored and faithful general agent, who put his heart

---

[16] "To the Friends of the Fugitive," *The Liberator*, October 18, 1850,

in his work."[17]

The unsung heroes mentioned in the mini-biographies above are just a fraction of the brave men and women involved in the Underground Railroad. Thousands of others will never be mentioned in history books, and still more that we haven't yet spoken of are famous.

In the following chapters, we will discuss more famous abolitionists and freedom seekers like Frederick Douglass. You may have noticed this chapter discussed only men who were part of the Underground Railroad. Coming up next, you'll hear about the brave women who risked their lives to both escape to freedom and help others, including the well-known Harriet Tubman, Sojourner Truth, Mary Ann Shad Cary, Harriet Beecher Stowe, and Ellen Craft.

---

[17] *The Liberator*, December 29, 1865.

Chapter 3: The Role of Safe Houses and Secret Codes

One aspect that adds intrigue and excitement to the tales of narrow escape and secret journeys to freedom are the details surrounding secret codes and stories of hidden "safe" rooms in homes all along Underground Railroad routes.

Over time, these details have become fantastical tall tales, adding to the Hollywood aspect of the more popular stories. What is true, and what's mythical? It can be difficult to differentiate at times. In some cases, there are excellent written records and first-hand accounts, and in other cases, history has been muddied by propaganda and lore.

One of the most prevalent myths about secret codes revolves around the use of symbolism sewn into quilts that were hung up for freedom seekers and abolitionists to see outside Underground Railroad safe houses. The basic idea of the "quilt code" is that the patterns of shapes often seen in patchwork quilts were used to signal messages.

The meaning of the patterns, the ways people along the Underground Railroad used the quilts and even who specifically used these quilts are not clear. A comprehensive study of the "quilt code" found that there were at least fifteen different widely known versions of the story. Not a single person has been able to give direct evidence of quilts being used; neither has anyone been able to name an ancestor who utilized codes from quilts on their journey north to freedom. It seems the only information is just a story someone told and passed on.

You might say, "Well, sometimes that's how oral history works." Oral history is based on stories shared between friends and family members, right?

Historians have studied further and found that some elements used in these "code quilt" stories were quilting patterns that came into use in the 1930s, well after the Underground Railroad ceased operations. Even the descriptions of African symbols on the quilts and their uses clash with the meanings of actual African symbols, making the "code quilt" idea even more fantastical.

Using quilts to convey escape routes or warnings seems to have been a nice idea to soften the blow of the brutal reality of travel along the Underground Railroad. The idea of code quilts makes a nice children's book and adds a feel-good element to the perilous journey north.

In reality, we do know of several documented uses of codes for travelers and abolitionists.[18] These codes were in the form of keywords used in letters. An "agent" was the person who was coordinating the escape. This person would make the plans, plot the travel on the map, and line up contacts along the route. The "conductor" was the person escorting the enslaved people, though we now know many people escaped on their own, fleeing north without a conductor to guide them. An "operator" could be either a conductor or an agent. The "drinking gourd" referred to the Big Dipper constellation and the North Star, which pointed freedom seekers northward without a conductor to guide them. "Baggage" referred to the fugitive enslaved people, the freedom seekers who were being transported by the Underground Railroad. "Bundles of wood" were the number of freedom seekers that should be expected to arrive. Canada was referred to as "Canaan" or "the Promised Land." The Ohio River was renamed the "River Jordan." The "gospel train" or the "freedom train" were both alternate names for the Underground Railroad. A "station" was a safe house, owned or run by a "station master."

Songs as Guides

Coded songs are another well-known part of the Underground Railroad's history taught in most schools in the United States as part of US history courses. First, students might learn about Harriet Tubman and her role in the Underground Railroad, guiding people to freedom.

---

[18] Underground Railroad Secret Codes: Harriet Tubman

Next, students might be introduced to a story about codes shared through songs that helped travelers and freedom seekers know where to go and when to travel and inspired them on their journey.

The best-known of these songs is called "Follow the Drinking Gourd."

According to H.B. Parks, an amateur folklorist, there was a man named Peg Leg Joe who traveled between plantations. Peg Leg Joe was a laborer, but this was just a cover for his actual purpose, which was to share the drinking gourd song with enslaved people around Mobile, Alabama.

The lyrics to the song are coded instructions for escaping. They give a verbal map that freedom seekers could follow to the north. First, the coded lyrics instruct people to leave Mobile and go up the Tombigbee River, then cross to find the Tennessee River. From there, they should travel down the river to Paducah, Kentucky. This is the spot where the Tennessee and Ohio rivers meet each other.

The lyrics are as follows:

"When the Sun comes back
And the first quail calls
Follow the Drinking Gourd.
For the old man is a-waiting for to carry you to freedom
If you follow the Drinking Gourd.

The riverbank makes a very good road.
The dead trees will show you the way.
Left foot, peg foot, traveling on,
Follow the Drinking Gourd.

The river ends between two hills
Follow the Drinking Gourd.
There's another river on the other side
Follow the Drinking Gourd.

When the great big river meets the little river
Follow the Drinking Gourd.
For the old man is a-waiting for to carry you to freedom
If you follow the drinking gourd."

The "Drinking Gourd" is also a code name for the constellation we now call the Big Dipper, which always points to the bright North Star. Following the constellation on a dark night was an easy way for people to know they were heading in the right direction if they were lost or unsure. The song told people to follow dead trees if it was too cloudy outside and there were no stars in the sky. This is because moss always grows on the north side of a decaying tree, signaling which direction to continue traveling.

H.B. Parks claims that the lyrics of "Follow the Drinking Gourd" were explained to him by a Black informant who detailed the secretive workings of the Underground Railroad. Parks also said that he himself heard the song three times, in three different places: in North Carolina in 1912, in Louisville in 1913, and in Texas in 1918.

The idea that an African American-style spiritual song contained a hidden verbal map exploded in popularity across the United States during the years after the Civil War as stories and tales about the Underground Railroad began to surface and books were published about the subject. This included a significant number of books with stories containing the song "Follow the Drinking Gourd." The stories about the song and the coded quilts have been enshrined in American culture, spread for years by popular children's books, movies, and the elementary teachers' lesson plans.

Recent research shows no factual basis for the existence of Peg Leg Joe or the use of this song as a map for escape. In fact, the story of Peg Leg Joe was first published in 1928, and the song was published by a white man named Lee Hays, of The Weavers quartet, in 1947! This leads us to ask if any songs said to have been sung along the Underground Railroad were truly utilized as secret coded signals. The answer to that seems to be a cautious yes, though this use was not nearly as prevalent as we have been led to believe by our third-grade teachers or popular children's books and movies.

Harriet Tubman possibly used two songs in her efforts to lead people to freedom. These were the songs "Go Down Moses" and "Bound for the Promised Land." Harriet Tubman herself has said she changed the tempo of these songs to indicate whether it was safe to come out of hiding.

"Wade in the Water" is another song that has been attributed to Harriet Tubman and the Underground Railroad. There is no definite proof this song was used. However, the lyrics were meant to instruct freedom seekers to get in the water so that the slave catcher's bloodhounds were unable to follow their scent and find them. The song has been included in countless albums and concerts featuring African spirituals, including the first commercial recording by Paramount Pictures in 1925 and a famous version by The Staple Singers that became part of the later civil rights movement.

As for other popular songs attributed to the Underground Railroad, their use during this time appears to be only a legend. For example, "Swing Low, Sweet Chariot" was written by an Afro-Cherokee Native American living in Oklahoma well after the Civil War. Harriet Tubman had never heard that song.

So great was the danger for enslaved people that they told no one except their closest friends and family that they planned to leave. There were no group announcements at meetings or word spread through entire plantations that Harriet Tubman was going to arrive. That would have been far too risky since the message could have been overheard or shared by someone willing to give away the escapee's plans to the enslaver.

Untangling the truth about the songs and codes used along the Underground Railroad can be difficult. However, historians today can find significant information from antebellum antislavery newspapers, as well as firsthand accounts from the many narratives written by enslaved people who escaped to freedom.

After the Civil War ended, people could speak freely about their experiences with the Underground Railroad because there was no longer any fear of punishment. In all the historical documents, news articles, books, and lectures, historians have never discovered any mention of coded quilts, secret tunnels, or even exciting hiding places other than your typical dark barn corner or dusty attic.[19]

Safehouses

The stories, books, and movies that have given us our impression of the Underground Railroad have been largely based in the South, giving us the idea that the Underground Railroad was an amazing network of well-hidden resources that spanned the Southern slave-holding states.

This is actually quite far from the truth. When escaping the South, enslaved people were largely on their own. Today, we can look back at a map and see the known safehouses and abolitionist locations across both

---

[19] "Opinion | History's Tangled Threads - The New York Times"

the North and the South. The map gives us a clear picture of what was happening during the operation of the Underground Railroad.

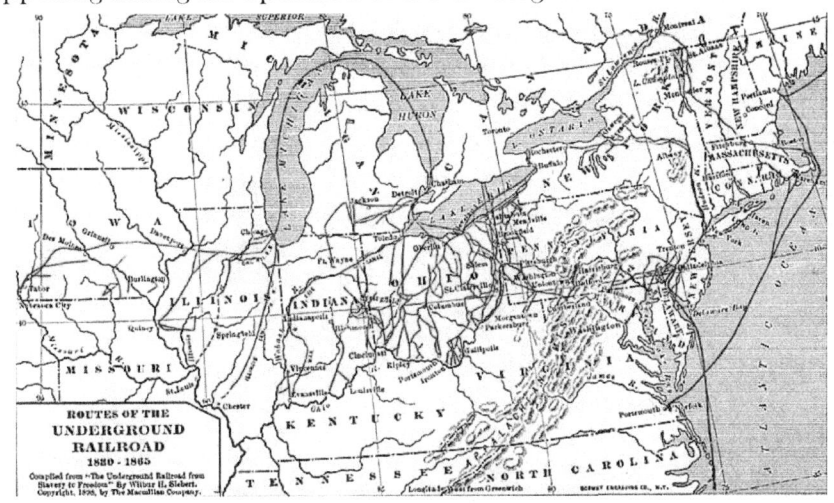

Map of Underground Railroad routes.
https://commons.wikimedia.org/wiki/File:Undergroundrailroadsmall2.jpg

For example, in the deep Southern state of Georgia, the official list of safehouses and meeting places has a total of two sites.[20] Yes, that's correct. In the entire state, there were only two places: the First African Baptist Church in Savannah and the Dr. Robert Collins house in Macon, which was used by William and Ellen Craft.

Were there more places we aren't aware of? That is quite possible, but the narratives and news articles only speak of these two places. For Black men and women trying to flee Georgia, this meant they were running through the state without any help. There was no secret network of homes with quilts hanging outside to guide them.

In the Southern slave state of North Carolina, there were also two official sites—the Guilford College Woods meeting place on the campus of Guilford College in Greensboro and the Freedmen's Colony of Roanoke Island on the Outer Banks.

We find the same situation in Tennessee. There are only two known safehouses there, as well: Burkle Estate, which is now the Slave Haven Underground Railroad Museum in Memphis, and the Hunt-Phelan house in Memphis.

---

[20] "A Tour Of The Underground Railroad - Georgia Tourism Board"

A few of the upper Southern states and areas, such as Washington, D.C., and Maryland, had a little more organization available to help fleeing enslaved people, but most of the Deep South did not contain any sort of secret network to aid fugitives on the run from their enslavers.

Enslaved people in Tennessee fled to Kentucky and found the Ohio River largely on their own, risking their lives to cross the wide, turbulent river under the cover of darkness. Today, most of the Ohio River has such a strong current that locals know it's a deadly place to swim.

In contrast, on the other side of the Ohio River, the Underground Railroad roared to life. History shows us that the Underground Railroad existed primarily in the northern states. The North did have a well-connected informal network of abolitionists, conductors and agents, safehouses, and even offices.

While there are only two historically known safehouses and abolitionist sites in Tennessee, do you know how many there are in Ohio? There are eighteen locations throughout Ohio, from the towns bordering the Ohio River all the way to the Great Lakes area in the northernmost part of the state.

New York state, which is a relatively small geographical area in comparison to Georgia or even Tennessee, has thirty known abolitionist and safehouse locations, revealing an intricate network of Underground Railroad support for freedom seekers. Another geographically small state, Pennsylvania, has fifteen locations within its borders. New Jersey has nine safehouses, and Massachusetts has twelve.

As mentioned earlier, the "Grand Central Station" of the Underground Railroad was a popular safehouse located in Fountain City, Indiana—the home of Levi Coffin, who was often referred to as the unofficial president of the Underground Railroad. Did you catch that? The most popular safehouse that helped more than 2,000 escapees wasn't in a slaveholding state in the South. It was across the Ohio River in Indiana.

You may be wondering why these safehouses were needed in the northern states. The safehouses were simply resting places and shelter, offered generously by abolitionists who wished to provide hospitality and assistance to those who were traveling farther north. In most cases, especially before the Fugitive Slave Act of 1850, these homes weren't hiding anyone.

Between the years of the Fugitive Slave Act of 1850 and the Civil War, angry "owners" did show up in the northern states to search for their "property" along the network of Underground Railroad houses. These were the instances when someone needed to be hidden. A few homes with secret rooms have been uncovered in border states. For example, in Salem, Ohio, several historical homes have secret rooms that can only be accessed with a ladder. Their use on the Underground Railroad has been verified by the personal journals of the homeowners, which are held by the local historical society.

The northern safe houses and meeting locations were so well known that they were sometimes advertised in local papers. For example, Jermaine Loguen, the Black leader of the Underground Railroad in Syracuse, regularly published his address as a place that welcomed fugitive slaves, offering them food and shelter.

The myths of the Underground Railroad give people what they want to hear. Everyone enjoys a good story with a hero or heroine, mysterious tunnels, and safe rooms. A network of concealed Southern safe houses revealed to freedom seekers only by coded songs and colorful quilts gives us easily understood and entertaining history we can share with our children. But this romanticized version of the Underground Railroad conceals the gritty and painful truth about the life and death struggle enslaved people faced, something many people may not want to hear or understand.

As the United States continues to strive toward equal rights for all people, many activists say it's time we stop sharing the myths of the Underground Railroad, which have been called a "national fairy tale" under the guise of "truth and justice for all," and instead teach our children the truth about slavery's history in the United States.

"Those who fail to learn history are doomed to repeat it," as the famous quote says.

Chapter 4: Stories of Great Bravery

The greatest figures of the Underground Railroad were those who made dangerous escapes from their enslavers in the South. Even though they were born with every disadvantage in life, they were strong enough to stand up and forge their own path. They fought back against oppression, teaching themselves how to read and write and going on to become powerful historical and political figures in the history of both the abolition movement and the United States.

Frederick Douglass

Frederick Douglass.
https://commons.wikimedia.org/wiki/File:Frederick_Douglass_(circa_1879).jpg

Almost everyone has heard the name Frederick Douglass. He was an abolitionist, an orator, and the author of his autobiography titled *Narrative of the Life of Frederick Douglass*. He was an excellent speaker, so much so that he became known as the spokesman for the abolitionist movement and the face of those who fought for racial equality.

How did an uneducated man, born as an enslaved person in the South, not only make it to freedom but also become so successful in his efforts that he became a household name?

At twenty-three years old, the recently freed Douglass found himself standing before a crowd of abolitionists who had traveled from long distances to hear him speak in Nantucket, Massachusetts. He was trembling with nerves and fear. In his narrative, he describes this moment:

"It [speaking publicly against slavery] was a severe cross, and I took it up reluctantly. The truth was, I felt myself a slave, and the idea of speaking to white people weighed me down. I spoke but a few moments, when I felt a degree of freedom, and said what I desired with considerable ease"[21]

This moment was the catalyst that launched Frederick Douglass into fame. His speech was emotional, raw, and stirring, describing his life as an enslaved person. The audience was deeply moved, and from then on, he became a sought-after speaker.

Frederick Douglass was born "Frederick Augustus Washington Bailey" in February 1818. He was unlucky enough to be born in the slaveholding state of Maryland as a Black person. His mother was also enslaved, and his father was an unnamed white man. He was enslaved at the same location as his grandparents and his aunt, while his mother worked in a forced labor camp far away. Douglass only saw her a handful of times in his young life because she died when he was seven years old.

During the first eight years of his life, Douglass experienced the complete degradation of slavery. He witnessed beatings and harsh punishments and saw families ripped apart as members were sold far away. He spent many nights cold and hungry when his enslavers didn't meet his basic needs.

---

[21] Douglass, Frederick : *Narrative of the Life of Frederick Douglass*.

Douglass was only an infant when he was separated from his mother. He would spend the first six of his life living with his maternal grandmother, Betty Bailey. However, things took a decidedly harsher turn when he was sent away from the only family he'd ever known to go work on the Wye Plantation in Maryland at just six years old.[22]

Sometime later, Frederick was "given" to Thomas and Lucretia Auld. This sense of stability in the boy's life was short-lived, as he was soon passed onto Thomas's brother in Baltimore, Hugh Auld, who was a ship captain. In many ways, this was life-changing for Frederick Douglass. He is quoted as saying that being sent to Baltimore "laid the foundation, and opened the gateway, to all my subsequent prosperity."[23]

Once in Baltimore, the young Douglass began taking in everything he could learn from the city around him. He quickly realized that reading and writing were necessary. Literacy was a gift given to all white people, but it was illegal for Black men and women to learn. Douglass decided to quietly teach himself to read using the things he saw around him in the city.

For seven years, Douglass enjoyed life in Baltimore. At age twelve, he reached another milestone. Douglass purchased his first book: a collection of writings titled *The Columbian Orator*. The subject happened to be a man's natural rights, and it included debates, essays, and radical speeches that filled Douglass with curiosity and ideas. The connection between freedom and literacy was well underway in the mind of Frederick Douglass. This smart, strong Black boy was exactly what enslavers disliked the most, as this endangered their way of life.

At this point in Douglass's short life, things took a turn for the worse. Ripped away from the big city of Baltimore, he was sent back to the eastern shore of Maryland at age fifteen to work on a farm run by a man named Edward Covey. Covey was notorious for being a "slave breaker." On this farm, Douglass experienced the daily horrors of being enslaved firsthand. He was whipped and beaten daily. He was starved and forced to do hard manual labor with almost no food. He was cold and dirty. He described himself as "broken in body, soul, and spirit."

This didn't stop Douglass from doing all he could to fight back against injustice. He quietly educated the other enslaved people around

---

[22] Frederick Douglass - History.com
[23] Frederick Douglass PBS Biography

him and physically fought back against the slave breaker.

On January 1, 1836, Frederick Douglass made a New Year's Resolution. He planned to be free by the time the year ended. Sadly, his bold and daring plan was found out, and he experienced more brutality while jailed for his escape attempt.

Frustrated with his troublemaking behavior, the enslaver sent Douglass back to Baltimore, where he worked in a shipyard. It was during this time in Baltimore that Douglass met his future wife, Anna Murray. She was a free Black woman. Anna risked her own freedom and safety to purchase a train ticket for Douglass. The new escape plan was for Douglass to dress like a sailor and calmly board a train for the free state of New York.

He boarded a train headed north on September 3, 1838. In a short twenty-four hours, Douglass had gone from being enslaved to being a free man in New York City. Anna met him once he was safe in the city, and they got married.

The couple feared being taken back to Maryland from New York City since there were many human traffickers in the area looking to make money. They decided to move further north to New Bedford, Massachusetts, where they took the last name Douglass and began a family. They had five children together: Rosetta, Lewis, Frederick, Junior, Charles, and Annie.

Douglass secured a job as a laborer, but he also pursued more education. He never wanted to stop learning. One of the first things he did was to join a Black church and begin to attend abolitionist meetings. He took out a subscription to *The Liberator*, mentioned several other times in this book.

The Liberator was a weekly abolitionist publication written by white abolitionist William Lloyd Garrison. In 1841, Frederick Douglass saw Garrison giving a lecture at the Bristol Anti-Slavery Society during their yearly meeting. Garrison gave a passionate speech expressing a deep hatred for the institution of slavery, which caught Douglass's attention and left a long-lasting impression.

In return, Garrison mentioned Douglass in *The Liberator* just a few days before Douglass gave his first powerful speech in front of the Massachusetts Anti-Slavery Society in Nantucket, drawing more people to the upcoming event. Those who heard the speech described it as both horrifying and heart-piercing. As a result of Douglass's speech, the

Massachusetts Anti-Slavery Society asked him to become a lecturer. He was given a three-year contract, which launched his lifelong career.

Douglass took speaking tours across the North and the Midwest, spreading knowledge about the way enslaved people were being treated in the South. He was so eloquent and well-spoken that people accused him of never being enslaved.

In 1845, he worked up the courage to publish his life's story, *Narrative of the Life of Frederick Douglass, an American Slave, Written by Himself.* This was a big risk for him because he named his enslavers, spoke of his escape, and gave personal details that could risk his freedom.

To maintain the safety of his family, they moved across the ocean to England for two years. Douglass toured England, Ireland, and Scotland, where he continued to share his story at various speaking events, selling many copies of his narrative along the way.

To protect Douglass, abolitionists purchased his freedom. This allowed the family to return to the United States, where Douglass walked back onto American soil a completely free man. The family moved to Rochester, New York, where Douglass began ardently working as a conductor with the Underground Railroad, helping many people on their journey north. He also became involved in the women's rights movement.

Until this time, William Lloyd Garrison had been a mentor to Frederick Douglass. While overseas, Douglass had continued learning and developing his own point of view, and he began to disagree with Garrison on certain key points. This was important because Frederick Douglass had a strong influence on the abolitionists of the time, which, in turn, swayed the political narrative.

Garrison was a radical abolitionist, meaning he spoke against churches and many political parties and even disagreed with voting. Garrison wanted the Union (the United States) to be dissolved. He was not in favor of a United States where slavery was outlawed in every state. Garrison also spoke out against the US Constitution, calling it pro-slavery.

In 1851, Douglass was ready to separate from Garrison. He spoke at an abolitionist meeting in Syracuse, New York, announcing that he believed the US Constitution was not pro-slavery. He firmly believed that the areas of the Constitution under the jurisdiction of the federal government supported emancipation, and he was in favor of a completely united country where the institution of slavery was outlawed federally. He felt that dissolving the Union would leave enslaved people abandoned and trapped in the Southern states with no hope of ever escaping to freedom.

Garrison and Douglass, while one-time allies who respected each other, strongly disagreed about many issues. During the years they knew each other, their views became more and more at odds on topics. Garrison, like many critics, felt that Douglass sounded "too educated" for an ex-slave. Instead, he should "dumb it down" to appeal to white audiences. In later years, Garrison opposed Douglass's plans to open a newspaper, feeling he was a better speaker and should not be wasting his time editing. Ultimately, it is believed both Garrison's and Douglass's views on abolition began to differ greatly as time went on. Garrison's intent was to never use violence in the anti-slavery movement, while Douglass began to view violence as acceptable when necessary. In particular, he said he believed that violent resistance to slave-catchers was "wise as well as just," a far cry from Garrison's beliefs.[24] Many believe this widening gap between views, even though both men ultimately had the same goal, is what drove them apart.

In 1855, Douglass published *My Bondage and My Freedom*, which was an expansion of his first narrative. In this book, Douglass continued to challenge the idea of slavery and brought up the growing issue of racial segregation in the northern United States.

When the fight for the end of slavery broke out into a physical war, Frederick Douglass never backed down. He recruited Black men to fight in the 54th Massachusetts Volunteer Infantry. His own sons fought, as well. Douglass had many connections and some political sway at this point. He spoke to President Abraham Lincoln to advocate for Black troops when he discovered they weren't getting equal pay and treatment.

As the war progressed, it looked like the North would win. But what would happen to the formerly enslaved people if slavery was outlawed across all states? Douglass began a new fight: the right for all Black people to have rights equal to those of white people as full American citizens. Politically, Douglass used his influence to get changes made to the US Constitution. The Thirteenth Amendment was ratified in 1865.

---

[24] University Of Rochester Frederick Douglass Project.

It abolished slavery at the federal level, which is exactly what Frederick Douglass had hoped for.

It wasn't until a few years later, in 1868, that Black people were granted national birthright citizenship with the Fourteenth Amendment. In 1870, the Fifteenth Amendment was ratified, stating that no one could be denied the right to vote based on their race, skin color, or previous status as an enslaved person.

By 1872, Frederick Douglass was a well-known public figure. The family moved to Washington, D.C., where Douglass continued advocating for equal rights. The United States entered the Reconstruction period after the Civil War, and many changes took place both in the government and in society. Douglass was appointed to prestigious positions in multiple committees and universities, even becoming a legislative council member of the District of Columbia Territorial Government.

Times continued to be tough for Black Americans. Racism and racial violence were at an all-time high. Black people were not always welcomed as members of government or high-ranking officers, and they faced physical assault, lies, and fraud in attempts to oust them from office. Douglass never gave up. He served with five United States presidents. He was the US Marshal for the District of Columbia from 1877 to 1881 and its Recorder of Deeds from 1881 to 1886. Douglass was also the minister resident and consul-general to Haiti from 1889 to 1891.

Douglass worked without ceasing until his very last day. On February 20, 1895, Douglass spent the morning at a meeting for the National Council of Women. He then went back to his home in Washington, D.C., to rest before giving a speech at a nearby church later in the afternoon. Shortly after, he suffered a sudden heart attack and died at his home. He was seventy-seven years old.

Born as an enslaved person, denied the right to an education, whipped, starved, and sold away from his family, Douglass had no advantages in life. In fact, as a boy, he had everything possible working against him. Yet, somehow, he managed to become a well-educated speaker and author, as well as one of the fiercest abolitionists and advocates for freedom and equality. He never wavered in the face of opposition, showing incredible bravery and resolve.

Frederick Douglass played an essential role in the Underground Railroad. He served as an inspirational figure, educating hundreds of other abolitionists, providing guidance, and bringing people together for the cause. Without Douglass, the entire outcome of Black rights after the Civil War could have been very different.

Ellen and William Craft

Ellen and William Craft.
https://commons.wikimedia.org/wiki/File:Ellen_and_William_Craft.png

Ellen and William Craft were just ordinary enslaved persons until, one day, they became brave enough to plan daring escapes from their homes on two different Georgia plantations. From there, they undertook a perilous journey with narrow escapes and even a stand-off with the US Marshals. Eventually, the couple ended up safe in England.

William Craft was born in 1824. His enslaver was known for being a kind, Christian man. William wryly commented later that his enslaver didn't think twice about selling his mother and father to two separate plantations in their old age, so distant that they never saw each other again. His enslaver then sold three of his siblings to different people, as well.

Due to this man's debt, the bank took possession of sixteen-year-old William and his fourteen-year-old sister. They were sold at auction, and William recalled crying silently as he watched his sister purchased by strangers and taken away. He never got the chance to say goodbye.

William ended up as an enslaved apprentice to a cabinet maker in Macon, Georgia. This job helped him build a valuable set of skills, though all his earnings went straight back to his enslaver. While he was working, he met the love of his life, Ellen Craft.

Ellen was born in 1826 on a nearby plantation in Clinton, Georgia, to an enslaved mother. Her father was the master of the plantation, Colonel James Smith. Ellen was very light-skinned. She was so pale, in fact, that people often mistook her for a member of the white family rather than an enslaved girl.

When Ellen was eleven, she was given as a wedding gift to the daughter of Colonel Smith's wife, who lived in Macon. It was there she met William, who was working as an apprentice.

In 1846, the couple was allowed to marry, but they were unable to live together because they had different enslavers. At first, they managed to live separately. Soon, they grew frustrated with the situation and decided to plan an escape to the North, where they could live in freedom as husband and wife.

Their idea for escape was unique and bold. Since Ellen had such light skin, they thought she could dress as a white man. William would act as her enslaved man. Ellen pretended to be ill, saying she was going to Philadelphia for medical care. She wrapped her head in a bandage and wore her arm in a sling. Wearing her arm in a sling served a second purpose as well: it hid her inability to write. Her bandaged head hid her face, which would clearly show she didn't have a beard.

The Crafts traveled by train and then by sea to reach Maryland. From there, they made their way to Philadelphia. In Philadelphia, they contacted an abolitionist group, which helped them on the rest of their journey. Ellen actually became ill while there and was nursed back to health by a Quaker family. After she was well enough to continue traveling, the couple moved further north to Boston, which had become the epicenter for abolitionists. Thankfully, Ellen could sew very well, and William was an excellent cabinet maker, so the two had no trouble supporting themselves in Boston. William opened his own successful cabinet shop at 51 Cambridge Street.

The Crafts decided to speak openly about their lives as enslaved people and their daring journey north. Like Frederick Douglass, they began giving speeches and lectures. Soon, they became well known. Various newspapers published their story, including The *New York Herald*, *The Boston Globe*, *The Georgia Journal*, and *The Macon Telegraph*.

The Crafts made their home on Beacon Hill in Boston, joining the robust community there and living at the house of Harriet and Lewis Hayden.

Everything was going very well for William and Ellen until the Fugitive Slave Act passed in 1850. Having seen their story in the newspaper, William and Ellen's previous enslavers sought a warrant for their arrest. Two slave catchers arrived in Boston to take the couple back into custody and return them to the Deep South.

Abolitionists from the League of Freedom quickly smuggled Ellen outside of the city to a safe place. William remained in his shop, arming himself before going back to the Hayden's home.

The slave catchers came to Lewis Hayden's home on Beacon Hill, but Lewis and William were prepared. They refused to open the door, saying that they had a keg of gunpowder with a fuse under the house and would light it if anyone set foot across the doorway. The slave catchers eventually gave up, deciding it wasn't worth risking their own lives to capture William.

The Crafts no longer felt safe in Boston. The abolitionist group helped them board a ship to England, where the slave catchers had no jurisdiction. Once in London, the couple had a family. They continued speaking out against slavery and telling their story. They published a book about their experiences called *Thousand Miles for Freedom; Or, the Escape of William and Ellen Craft from Slavery.*[25]

The abolitionist publication *The Liberator* wrote about William traveling to West Africa to meet with the King of Dahomey. There, *The Liberator* says, William showed the king "the superior advantages of peaceful and legitimate commerce over the atrocious slave-trade with its concomitant barbarities."[26]

After the Civil War ended, the Crafts decided it was safe to return to the United States. They raised money and purchased a plantation in South Carolina, which they turned into a co-op farm for freed enslaved people. They faced racial violence in the area, which escalated continually until the Ku Klux Klan burned down their plantation. The Crafts didn't give up. They moved back to an area just outside of Savannah, Georgia, where they opened their own school for children.

---

[25] William Craft (U.S. National Park Service)

[26] "Dahomey," *The Liberator* (Boston, Massachusetts), February 20, 1863, Genealogybank.

The school taught around seventy-five students at a time.

After more than ten years of operating their school, the Crafts faced economic hardship due to slander from white people in the community. Their school was unwelcome by white members of the community, who did everything they could to destroy the school's reputation and force Ellen and William out of the area.

They made the difficult decision to close the school and went to live with their daughter's family in Charleston, South Carolina, where they peacefully spent the rest of their lives.[27]

The Crafts' cunning escape from slavery and their refusal to be recaptured was an inspiring story that spread around the globe, catching the interest of abolitionists and the average person alike. Their story helped bring awareness to the situation of enslaved people, allowing abolitionists to share more with curious people.

Harriet Jacobs

Harriet Jacobs.
State Archives of North Carolina Raleigh, NC, No restrictions, via Wikimedia Commons; https://commons.wikimedia.org/wiki/File:Harriet_Jacobs.jpg)

Harriet Ann Jacobs was born in Edenton, North Carolina, in the fall of 1813. Harriet had a relatively happy childhood for an enslaved person. Her enslaver's wife was kind to her, teaching her how to read

---

[27]"Ellen Smith Craft | Georgia Women of Achievement."

and sew. Harriet recalled not knowing she was enslaved until she was six years old.

When her enslaver died in 1825, Harriet's good fortune changed. Based on her enslaver's will, Harriet was left to the woman's niece. The niece was only a three-year-old child at the time, so Harriet's care was given over to the girl's father, Dr. James Norcom. She was quickly introduced to the painful reality of life as an enslaved person. Unfortunately, though she was only a young teenager, Harriet quickly realized Dr. Norcom was a sexual threat to her. Harriet struggled to escape Dr. Norcom's advances the entire time she was in his household, from 1825 until 1842.

Harriet was hated by Dr. Norcom's wife, who was suspicious of her husband, and felt very alone, scared, and trapped by her situation. Out of desperation, she went to a white lawyer named Samuel Tredwell Sawyer. She ended up having two children with Samuel Sawyer before she was twenty years old. Feeling even more desperate, in 1835, Harriet came up with a plan to convince Dr. Norcom to sell her children to their father.

Harriet's grandmother was a free Black woman. Harriet decided to hide in the small crawl space above the storeroom at her grandmother's house, hoping to convince Dr. Norcom she had run away. The storeroom was a small seven-by-nine-foot space with a sloping ceiling and no natural light. Harriet only came out at night for exercise.

Shockingly, her plan worked, at least in a roundabout way. Dr. Norcom did sell her two children, Joseph and Louisa, to their father, the lawyer. In an attempt to gain a measure of revenge against Harriet, Dr. Norcom sold her children as well as her brother John to a slaver. Dr. Norcom demanded that the slaver sell the children and John to a different state. His goal was to separate the family as much as possible in a bid to cut at the heart of Harriet. The slaver who purchased Harriet's children and brother was in league with Sawyer. In a stroke of good fortune, the slaver sold Harriet and Sawyer's children to Sawyer.[28] Harriet spent seven long years hiding in that small storage space, keeping tabs on her children through a peephole she drilled to see outside her attic storeroom. She also wrote letters to Dr. Norcom, attempting to confuse him by acting like she was in different locations.

---

[28] Jacobs, Harriet A. *Incidents in the Life of a Slave Girl, Written by Herself: Electronic Edition*

In 1837, Sawyer was elected to the United States House of Representatives. He moved to Washington, D.C., leaving behind his children, which he owned as enslaved people. Harriet was heartbroken and decided to escape to the North.

In 1842, she fled, going north by boat. Her daughter, Louisa, was a house servant in Brooklyn, New York, having been sent there by her father to work. Dr. Norcom pursued Harriet through Boston and New York City for ten years, attempting to capture her and return her to slavery.

Eventually, Harriet reunited with her brother, who was a fugitive enslaved person living in Rochester, New York. She began working with abolitionists in the office above *The North Star*, a paper owned by the renowned Frederick Douglass.

Finally, an abolitionist friend purchased Harriet's freedom. Harriet no longer had the smothering burden of being a fugitive.

Harriet had the courage to write her own book, a narrative called *Incidents in the Life of a Slave Girl*. It was the first publication to freely speak of the sexual harassment of Black minor girls by their male enslavers.

Harriet continued to be an abolitionist and active participant in the fight for freedom and equality even after the Civil War. She used her popularity from the book to raise money for recently emancipated African Americans, and she worked tirelessly to improve the living conditions for those who were now free at last.

Chapter 5: The Fugitive Slave Act and Its Impact

As we've already discovered, in 1850, a monumental change occurred in the United States. The Fugitive Slave Act was passed.

As you may recall, before the Fugitive Slave Act of 1850, individual states decided for themselves whether they would be free states or allow the institution of slavery. An enslaved person could travel along the Underground Railroad, escaping their enslaver to freedom in the Northern states. Once in a Northern state, they would be relatively safe and free.

After the Fugitive Act of 1850, fugitives—that is, enslaved people on the run from their enslavers—could have a warrant for their arrest taken out by their former enslavers. This warrant allowed "slave catchers" to go into any state in the Union, even free states, to pursue the fugitives. Worse, the US Marshals and local police forces in free states were required to aid the slave catchers. This meant that no Black person who had been formerly enslaved was safe anywhere in the United States. They must now go all the way to Canada to be free.

Let's take a step back for one moment.

Before the Fugitive Slave Act of 1850, did Southern enslavers have any rights to men and women who escaped from them and headed north into free states? Or was the Fugitive Slave Act of 1850 the first law to give them these rights over freedom seekers outside of their state's lines?

The answer to this is somewhat complex and begins with the first thirteen colonies of the United States. We are all aware of the United States Constitution, that is, the document that describes how the United States government will operate and how the power will be distributed throughout the different branches of the government.

When the Thirteen Colonies defeated Britain in the Revolutionary War, they were thirteen very separate communities with different geographies, industries, and people living in them. They were united by a single goal: freedom from control by a foreign government—that is, freedom from Britain.

After the colonies found themselves free, they decided to attempt to unite the colonies into one country. When drafting the Constitution, they were forced to acknowledge that slavery existed in several of the colonies. Not only did it exist, but it was essential to the culture and economy of these colonies.

To move ahead and create a new nation, they decided to postpone one very important decision: whether this would be a nation that accepted slavery. To skirt around that decision, slavery was not directly mentioned in the Constitution. Instead, it was implied with indirect wording.

Article 4, Section 2, Clause 3 of the Constitution clearly explains that if an enslaved person or an indentured servant escapes from his "owner" and runs to another state, the law requires that this person be returned to their original "owner." This element of the Constitution was an important piece that sealed together the two groups of colonies: those with enslaved people and those without. Article 4, Section 2, Clause 3 was meant to solve a border problem occurring between the two types of colonies. It was an extradition treaty of sorts.

Without this agreement, the signers of the Constitution could not have finalized the new nation. Those in the Southern colonies had to be reassured that they would not risk having to give up their property by joining the United States. So, the newly birthed United States arrived with a hint of slavery built into its founding document.

Throughout the first forty years of the nineteenth century, free states in the North followed this article of the Constitution in different ways. It left a lot open to interpretation. Many free Northern states added different "personal freedom" laws into their state legislation. These laws supported free Black men and women and fugitive escapees who made their homes in free states.

As the Underground Railroad grew more successful, more and more enslaved people began to make their way north. Tensions began to rise until 1842 when things came to a head. At the time, Pennsylvania had the strictest personal liberty law of any free state. It gave the best protection to Black people living within its state borders. This personal liberty law was suddenly challenged in the Supreme Court in a case called *Prigg v. Pennsylvania*.

The chief justice of the Supreme Court was Justice Story, who was against slavery. Story also felt backed into a corner because he had vowed to uphold the Constitution in his rulings. This led to the overturning of Pennsylvania's personal liberty law. Story ruled that any law interfering with the fugitive slave clause in the Constitution, Article 4, Section 2, Clause 3, must be struck down. The Constitution would take precedence over state laws. This federal ruling overturned all the personal liberty laws that had been passed in free Northern states over the first part of the nineteenth century.

Now you might be wondering what the difference is between Article 4, Section 2, Clause 3 of the Constitution and the Fugitive Slave Act of 1850. That is an excellent question. The clause in the Constitution that Justice Story ruled as overriding the personal liberty laws made by states did not include any specific directions for how these fugitive enslaved people were to be returned to their "owners" in the South. This part was completely left up to interpretation.

Instead of solving this border issue between the Northern and Southern states, *Prigg v. Pennsylvania* added more fuel to the flames as disagreements and tension continued to rise. The invisible Underground Railroad was chugging along steadily north, speeding the North and the South toward inevitable violence.

At this point, the Fugitive Slave Act of 1850 entered the scene during what is referred to as the Compromise of 1850. Congress struggled to maintain that the United States was actually one happy country, while the ever-growing fugitive slave issue pulsed through every Northern and Southern city. Their solution was the Fugitive Slave Act of 1850.

We can see how the Fugitive Slave Act was meant to bring an end to the confusion left behind by the *Prigg v. Pennsylvania* case. The Fugitive Slave Act was specific, outlining how fugitives would be returned to the South and explaining who was to aid in their capture and return.

For many white Northerners, the Fugitive Slave Act was a startling wake-up call to the horrors of slavery. They had been living alongside Black people in freedom for many years. Some white Northerners had no issue with the Black members of society, while others were uncomfortable. However, none were prepared for the harsh realities they were about to witness with the passing of the Fugitive Slave Act.

First and foremost, assisting a formerly enslaved person was now a federal crime. This meant that abolitionists risked committing federal crimes daily. White allies now had to choose whether they wanted to be involved at great risk to themselves and their families or remain silent.

Moreover, the Fugitive Slave Act required private citizens to help locate missing slaves if they were ordered to do so. If they didn't want to help and refused, they would have to pay large fines. This forced white Northerners to become involved in slavery even when they wanted to remain quietly on the sidelines without picking a side.

Free Black men and women could be accused of a federal crime for helping their friends and family make it north or for keeping them safe once they arrived. For free Black people, the Fugitive Slave Act was terrifying. Unless they could show papers stating they were emancipated, they were at risk of being kidnapped by human traffickers and taken South, where they could be sold or given to anyone who claimed to have owned them.

Anxiety in the Black communities was through the roof. Boston had been a proud center of freedom and liberty for many years, but now? The city was being told by the government that it must participate in sending its citizens back to a cruel life of slavery.

The Fugitive Slave Act went much further than the clause in the Constitution by denying accused fugitives the right to trial by jury. In free cities like Syracuse and Boston, white citizens witnessed Black citizens being hunted down, chained, and dragged off to court. For the first time, people in the North witnessed their Black neighbors being held in chains in a courtroom, denied the right to defend themselves or even speak. People in the North were shocked and offended by the sight of Black people being treated like objects or animals.

After court, people saw these so-called fugitives being shoved onto boats and shipped away to the South, never to return.

To have these things done in your own neighborhood in front of your children by strangers from the Deep South was very jarring. Then, to be told you would be committing a federal crime if you tried to stop the horrific treatment? This really hammered home just how vile the institution of slavery was. Many Northerners who had resisted abolitionists and preferred not to think about slavery before now had their eyes wide open for the first time. There was no turning back.

If the Fugitive Slave Act sought to give clarity, it had succeeded, just not in the way intended. The clarity came to people in the North like a shock: Slavery was not a Southern problem. It was an issue for the entire United States that would have to be addressed, and quickly.

People who had previously thought slavery had nothing to do with them in the North began to understand how the entire United States participated in the enslavement of human beings. Not only were they seeing their Black neighbors forcibly returned to the South, but they were also beginning to realize that the cotton they used in their clothing was grown and harvested by enslaved people in the South. The banks they invested their money in also participated in plantation ownership where people were enslaved. Ending slavery would change things for the entire country's economy, but people realized they could no longer silently participate in such heinous acts.

The Fugitive Slave Act was the fatal blow that pushed the United States closer to war between free states and Southern states. Violence began breaking out in the Northern states as slave owners and slave catchers showed up to reclaim what they viewed as their property.

Abolitionists were furious at the situation. They vowed to use civil disobedience whenever possible to resist this new law. One of the first and most notable tests of how the new law would work out came in September 1851.

Christiana, Pennsylvania, was home to six Black people who had been enslaved by the same man. This enslaver arrived boldly in the free state of Pennsylvania to claim his slaves based on his rights in the Fugitive Slave Act of 1850. He brought a group of men to help him capture his slaves and return them to his home in the South.

Having gotten word of the enslaver's arrival, a local group was already protecting the six fugitives in a home in the area. There was a tense argument between the two sides that quickly turned violent. As many as fifty Black men from the surrounding area showed up to help the group protect the fugitives. The enslaver and his men requested that local white men help them in the fight, as they were required to do by the Fugitive

Slave Act, but everyone refused. A violent riot broke out, and the enslaver was killed.

Five white men, along with thirty-eight Black men, were arrested and charged with treason against the United States, which was an offense punishable by death. The first man's trial was long and tense, lasting three weeks. In the end, each man was found not guilty, and the charges were dropped.

The abolitionists felt victorious. The law was on the side of morality in their eyes, as those who had disobeyed the Fugitive Slave Act were ultimately found not guilty.

As you've seen in the biographies of brave and famous men and women who participated in the Underground Railroad, the Fugitive Slave Act affected every Black person who thought they had found freedom and safety in a Northern free state. The Underground Railroad now needed to extend further than safe havens like Boston or Philadelphia. Now the goal for freedom seekers was an even more dangerous journey all the way to the Canadian border.

What began to happen was a complete breakdown of the United States federal government.

On one side were radical abolitionists who sounded extremely offensive to Southern enslavers. Many of these people had inherited their enslaved people. They were religious and felt that they were kind, generous, and living a moral life within the bounds of their society. The words of abolitionists were shocking and harsh to their ears. On the other side, the anger of enslavers who faced threats to their livelihoods, entire culture, and way of life was unbelievable to the people in the North for whom slavery was not normalized.

Keep in mind this was supposed to be one united country. Both the North and South had men involved in politics who were becoming increasingly polarized over this issue of fugitive people and the larger issue of how the nation could move forward with a united front if half of the country's economy and culture was held up by the power of human bondage.

To prevent the country from becoming completely authoritarian, the institution of slavery was too great of an issue for either side to compromise. Things came to a full boil when half the states seceded from the Union, leading to the Civil War in which nearly one million lives were lost.

In 1864, Congress repealed the Fugitive Slave Law. This was one year before the Civil War ended, but by this point, there was no one in the government to represent the South and vote against it.

Chapter 6: Religion and the Underground Railroad

To fully understand the role religion played in the abolitionist movement, we must first consider American society in the late 1700s through the 1800s, leading up to the Civil War. At this time, the country was firmly founded on Christian values.

Christianity created the basis for abolitionist beliefs and the moral struggle between helping enslaved people in defiance of the government or refusing to break the law and standing by while fellow humans were in bondage.

On the other hand, Southerners who owned enslaved people were also religious. For them, the Bible justified the ownership of slaves, and they felt they were well within their moral rights.

There is also a very important third aspect of religion in the nineteenth century that we will discuss: the point of view of enslaved people, who found religion to be an important part of their lives.

Quakers

The Quakers are the most prominent religious group attributed to the abolitionist movement, aside from Black men and women themselves. Most Quakers were white, though there were also Black Quakers who worked as abolitionists and agents on the Underground Railroad.

Quakers believe that God can be found within every human being. This includes absolutely everyone, from enslaved to free, with every color of skin and from every station in life.

Since Quakers believe every human is equally worthy of respect, unsurprisingly, this led to a direct objection to slavery. The Quakers began speaking out against slavery as early as the days of the thirteen colonies, well before the antebellum and Civil War periods. One of their first abolitionist groups was called The Society for the Relief of Free Negroes Unlawfully Held in Bondage, formed in Philadelphia in 1775.

The Quakers knew they needed to formally make a statement against the institution of slavery for their members. In 1780, they had come up with a plan and passed a Quaker law titled An Act for the Gradual Abolishment of Slavery. This made it illegal for members of the Quaker church to enslave people. They claimed no member should claim a human being as their own property. If a member continued to attempt to own another human being, they were "read out" from the meetinghouse. In other words, they were excommunicated.

The Quakers were the earliest church congregation to forbid its members to enslave people.

However, the Quakers faced a problem. The land in which they lived allowed for and even supported the practice of slavery. The Quakers strictly followed biblical teachings, which said, "Render therefore unto Caesar the things which are Caesar's; and unto God the things that are God's" (Matthew 22:21 KJV).

What were the Quakers to do in a case where, biblically, God demanded one thing (to not enslave others), and at the same time, the Bible also commanded them to follow the law of their land? They decided it was their duty to suffer the possible punishments that came from disobeying the law of the land rather than bring harm to other human beings.

Quaker William Jackson summed it up for his brethren when, in 1846, he said, "No one is under any moral obligation to lend himself as a tool to others for the commission of a crime, even when commanded by his government to do the wrong..."[29]

In fact, this was not the first time Quakers would be willing to face jail time when their beliefs contradicted those of their country's government. In the past, Quakers willingly went to jail for refusing to bear arms. In

---

[29] Densmore, Christopher, "Quakers and the Underground Railroad: Myths and Realities"

other cases, they were jailed for refusing to take an oath. These were forms of civil disobedience, which had been a Quaker practice for many years. Therefore, it is not a surprise that the Quakers would become determined abolitionists.

Not every Quaker was an abolitionist, but many did live side by side with the free Black population in places like New Jersey and Pennsylvania. The story of Thomas Mitchell is one such example of white Quaker families living closely with free Black people.

Thomas Mitchell was a fugitive Black man living in Chester County, Pennsylvania, only eighteen miles from the farm where he had been enslaved. He had been living as a fugitive for twelve years. One night after the Fugitive Slave Act of 1850, while he was sleeping in his bed, white slave catchers snuck up on his home and illegally kidnapped him. They took him straight to the slave market in nearby Baltimore, Maryland.

When questioned about committing a federal crime by not reporting the fugitive slave living next to them, Mitchell's white neighbors denied any knowledge. Likely, the area had many other Black people living freely as fugitives.

In the end, Mitchell's neighbors sought him out and purchased his freedom, returning him to his home where he had peacefully spent the last twelve years of his life.

One of the most famous white Quaker station masters on the Underground Railroad was named Thomas Garrett. Supposedly, Garrett assisted more than 2,700 people north to freedom from his home in Wilmington, Delaware. He owned an iron and hardware business at his home on 227 Shipley Street. Garett also welcomed travelers along the Underground Railroad to his home without question.

In 1848, Garett was arrested for helping the Hawkins Family, a Black family fleeing Maryland. As part of the conviction, he was fined $5,400. He ended up losing almost everything he owned, including his business and all his possessions.

The Baptists and Methodists

What about other branches of Christianity? Were there abolitionists and white allies that weren't Quakers? The answer to that question is absolutely yes. Both the Baptist and Methodist churches had white and Black members who were against slavery. Free Black congregations led by Black ministers were spreading across the North and even in

Southern states. Black ministers were delivering anti-slavery messages, bringing hope and inspiration to their congregations. It was their belief that slavery would be outlawed in their lifetime, and they spread this message through the church pulpit.

A "great revival" ministry sprang up in the South around Kentucky. This ministry encouraged white enslavers to free their enslaved people and called for slavery to be abolished. This led to many members of congregations manumitting, or giving freedom to, their slaves. White Methodist, Baptist, and Presbyterian churches sponsored Black church congregations filled with newly freed slaves.

Politically, these three branches of Christianity had different stances. The Methodists acknowledged the "evils of slavery" while at the same time announcing they were against "modern abolition." The Presbyterians stated that slavery was a legal and political matter and not something for the church to decide. The Baptists and the Methodists created regional denominations. This led to the formation of the Southern Baptist Convention.

There were many famous abolitionists, both Black and white, who were Methodist, Presbyterian, or Baptist. Harriet Tubman, for example, was a Methodist. African American churches quickly became places of refuge for those traveling along the Underground Railroad. Today, the map of buildings used as safehouses and meeting places across the United States is dotted with many Black churches, quite a few of which are still active today.

Religion for Enslaved People

For those who were enslaved, religion played several important roles. Africa is a large continent, and enslaved people were taken from many regions. Some of them were Muslim, already acquainted with the idea of a holy book and a monotheistic religion. Others had completely different religious traditions based on their tribes.

Almost all enslavers were Christian men. This meant that their enslaved people were quickly introduced to the Christian Bible. One of the main ways Christianity first spread among enslaved people was through song. This is where the Negro spiritual was born. Negro spirituals are songs that retell Bible stories and Christian concepts orally, which is how they were passed on from generation to generation. Since enslaved people were not allowed to read or write, the spiritual was their only way of sharing stories. The call-and-response style of worship was also born from the need to share religion without reading or writing. The worship leader would sing the first line of a song, and the people would repeat it.

Black enslaved people learned about the book of Exodus and saw it as a metaphor for their struggles. They focused on those stories as hope that they, too, would one day be freed.

On plantations, slaveholders would often bring in white preachers to deliver Sunday messages to the enslaved people. This allowed the enslavers to choose only messages that would support their claims that God upheld the idea of slavery. Meanwhile, for free Black people, the church was beginning to serve as a refuge. It was a place where they could learn to read and write, a place that would hide them from slave catchers, and a haven free from the daily onslaught of dehumanization from racist white people.

In all, the role of religion during this period in American history was so powerful that it bridged the gap between slaveholders, enslavers, and Quakers. Each group of people had a separate viewpoint, but all three used the Bible as their guide.

Chapter 7: The Impact of the Underground Railroad on African American Life

The migration of Black Americans from the slave states in the South to the free states in the North led to the creation of many unique Black communities in large Northern cities. Some of these communities include the historic Beacon Hill in Boston, Philadelphia, Cleveland, Detroit, and the ever-multicultural New York City.

Black citizens, both fugitive and legally free, fought for their right to have comfortable living spaces, well-paying jobs, and respect from their fellow white citizens. Black men became business owners, politicians, and activists in free states, which sharply contrasted with life for the enslaved Black men in the South.

Here are the stories of a few cities where Black people struggled and succeeded at creating their own communities.

Boston, Massachusetts

Boston, Massachusetts prides itself on being a city that represents liberty. It was the first city to fight back against British tyranny with the Boston Tea Party. It's only fitting that it would be a refuge for free Black men and women and the center of the abolitionist movement in the years leading to the Civil War.

Beacon Hill was home to the largest African American community in the United States during the nineteenth century. A mix of people made Beacon Hill their home. Many famous activists, political leaders, and religious leaders lived in the Beacon Hill neighborhood, including Louis and Harriet Hayden, John J. Smith, Abiel Smith, John Coburn, and William C. Neil. It was home to the Massachusetts State House, as well, drawing in many local politicians. Beacon Hill can be considered the place where the abolitionist movement was born, as well as the host to the largest number of Underground Railroad safe houses in the United States.

Families who lived in the Beacon Hill area worked together for common goals. They wanted to educate their children, create supportive institutions for recently escaped and freed people, and continually strive to achieve their goal of abolishing slavery in the United States.

In 1835, the Abiel Smith School in Beacon Hill was the first place in Boston that opened solely for the education of Black children. In 1855, Black Bostonians fought to integrate the public school system and won. The Phillips School in the Beacon Hill neighborhood became one of the very first integrated schools.

And the heartbeat of Beacon Hill? That was the existing Black church building, known today as the African Meeting House. It still stands in the Beacon Hill neighborhood and can be visited on a historic tour.

The Black community played a vital role in nineteenth-century Boston, having a strong influence on politics and bringing famous abolitionists to the local culture of the area.

Philadelphia, Pennsylvania

Philadelphia is in Pennsylvania, which was a free state that offered personal liberties to fugitive and free Black men and women within its state lines. Philadelphia was both an important location on the Underground Railroad and a racially charged place to live for fugitive and free Black citizens. The most pressing goal of the free Black people living in Philadelphia was to protect Black people from being taken back into slavery and guard them from the violence brought upon them by white people.

Slave catchers regularly came to the area looking for fugitive enslaved people, but they also kidnapped free Black people, as well. The need to protect the community from these people led to the formation of vigilance committees, which ended up playing an important role along the Underground Railroad in the North.

Philadelphia had a large population of free Black citizens. They worked alongside white allies, often Quakers, and both white and Black abolitionists to not only protect vulnerable people but also provide legal help. The Pennsylvania Abolition Society was an important part of the Philadelphia Black community.

The white community in Philadelphia was not entirely supportive of the growing number of Black residents, as more and more people arrived to live freely in the city. Black abolitionists often faced angry mobs of white citizens. When Black citizens found themselves successful economically, they were often attacked in an attempt to knock them back down.

Recently escaped or freed African Americans flocked to Philadelphia to find work in the large city. Unfortunately, they would often end up with the worst jobs and the lowest pay, competing against European immigrants for basic jobs. Black people were not included in the industrial job sector of the growing city, limiting them to physical labor and service jobs.

Despite this struggle, some Black citizens found creative ways to succeed. James Forten is a well-known Black businessman from Philadelphia who lived from 1766 to 1842. He started his own sail-making business and found amazing success on the waterfront, where many Black people worked on the docks at the most backbreaking, low-paying jobs.

Black people discovered a unique niche they could make their own in Philadelphia high society as highly skilled waiters and caterers, earning them both a good income and a measure of respect. Other Black citizens were well-known teachers, scholars, and ministers throughout the city, seeking to pass on education, knowledge, and inspiration to those who were struggling to better themselves.

Cleveland, Ohio

The free African American community in Cleveland was established in 1809 with the arrival of George Peake. From there, the community grew steadily. By 1860, the city had around 800 free Black citizens, though the Black population stayed around only 2 percent of the city's population.

Ohio sought to restrict free Black people from settling within the state and reduce the amount of fugitive freedom seekers taking refuge in its cities. The state passed laws known as "Black Laws" that required any Black person who lived in the state to pay a bond of $500. The person must also keep a document proving their free status with them at all times to show whenever asked.

Despite the harsh laws, Cleveland was one of the first cities in Ohio to have integrated public schools, beginning in the 1840s. Black citizens found success in many areas of the city. Some Black citizens became wealthy and enjoyed life as business owners in Cleveland, contributing to a multicultural city with many opportunities. They owned businesses such as real estate agencies, stores, hotels, restaurants, and barbershops.

The city's first Black-owned newspaper began in 1883. It was called *The Cleveland Gazette*. The first Black church didn't come until 1830 when St. John's African Methodist Episcopal Church opened. The second Black church, the Mt. Zion Congregational Church, wasn't established until a shocking thirty-four years later.

New York City, New York

New York City has been a home to African people since its earliest days as a Dutch colony. Throughout the city's history, various cultural groups have grown in numbers and then diminished due to migration, discrimination, and other historical factors.

The community of Weeksville was established in the 1830s in New York City. The goal of the settlement was to provide a social framework, help Black citizens gain economic stability and success, and help them gain political rights. Weeksville was located about four miles east of downtown Brooklyn.

By 1855, the little community had grown to a population of 521 Black people, making it the second-largest Black community in America with complete independence. The residents were people from both the United States and the Caribbean islands. The community was proud that Black citizens owned their own property. The city had two Black-owned newspapers called *Freedom's Torchlight* and the *National Monitor*. They also had their own churches, an orphanage, and an old folks' home.

Weeksville had the first public school with a multi-racial teaching staff and was the home of the first Black woman in New York to earn a medical degree. Dr. Susan McKinney Steward was born in Weeksville in

1847. She graduated from New York Medical College for Women in 1869 as the class valedictorian.[30]

Today, four homes remain as evidence of this vibrant Black community in New York City. They are located on Hunterfly Road and are cared for by the Weeksville Heritage Center.

Seneca Village was another well-known Black community in New York City during the nineteenth century. It was established in 1825 when a man named John Whitehead divided his estate and sold it off in small parcels.

Black New Yorkers realized the only way to gain political power in the city was to become landowners. New York State allowed Black men to vote if they owned more than $200 in real estate. The purchase of land for a Black man in Seneca Village offered both the chance to take part in a community and an opportunity to vote.

In 1855, tragedy struck the small community. By that time, many citizens had started small farms and gardens, churches and schools had been established, and the community was thriving. Mayor Wood used the power of eminent domain in the area, taking it for New York City property. The land was to be completely cleared of all the establishments so that the city could use it for a park. Black owners spent two years trying to fight the city before they were violently removed in 1857.

New York City itself is home to one of the lesser-known but most important abolitionists in the history of the Underground Railroad. David Ruggles came to New York at the age of seventeen. In 1835, he helped found the New York Committee of Vigilance. This group worked to protect Black citizens from slave catchers and white violence.

David Ruggles helped a startling 600 freedom seekers, including the famous Frederick Douglass. He provided hospitality and shelter to people in his own home on Lispend Street, which he used as a boarding house. From his home, Ruggles established a small bookstore and a library to make information easily accessible to Black people in his community. He distributed many anti-slavery booklets and pamphlets to further the cause of abolitionists.

Thomas Downing is another influential and well-known Black man who lived in New York City during the nineteenth century. He opened a

---

[30] "Weeksville - NYC's Early African American Settlements - Research Guides at New York Public Library Research Centers"

famous oyster house called Downings Oyster House on the corner of Broad Street and Wall Street. Customers at his oyster house included wealthy bankers and businessmen, politicians from the area, and even upper-class socialites. His restaurant served oysters that were either raw, stewed, or fried.

Perhaps the best part about Downing's Oyster House was not the oysters or the clientele but the happenings in the basement below the restaurant. The building was a stop on the Underground Railroad. Thomas Downing's son George took freedom seekers through the basement, helping them on their way to Canada.

Downing also played a major role in the creation of the United Anti-Slavery Society of the City of New York.

Another significant location on the Underground Railroad in New York City was the Colored Sailors' Home. It was located at the corner of Gold and John Streets, in lower Manhattan. The home was established by an abolitionist named William Powell. It served several purposes, including providing Black sailors with food and shelter, helping assist with employment opportunities, and as a meeting spot for abolitionists.

Most importantly, the Colored Sailor's Home helped around 1,000 enslaved people on their journey north. People were given food and shelter as they hid in the building from slave catchers. They were disguised as sailors and sent onward to the next stop.

Brooklyn's Plymouth Church was another site that earned the nickname "Grand Central Depot" for its significance along the Underground Railroad. It is still located today on 75 Hicks Street in Brooklyn, with an active church congregation.

The first minister of the church, Henry Ward Beecher, happened to be the sibling of the famous author Harriet Beecher Stowe, who wrote *Uncle Tom's Cabin*. The church hid fugitive Black men and women in the basement, and church members hosted people in their own homes at times.

Detroit

Detroit was a popular city for freedom seekers due to its location on the border with Canada. Many local citizens of Detroit participated in the Underground Railroad, giving shelter to people on the final stop of their journey to freedom. Slavery was abolished in Michigan in 1834.

Not everyone crossed the border into Canada. Some fugitive and free Black people stayed to make their home in Detroit. Some of the more famous people include drugstore owner Samuel C. Watson, William Whipper, Laura Haviland, and Henry Bibb.

The Black citizens of Detroit also participated in the Civil War. The 102nd Regiment United States Colored Troops of Michigan and Illinois took a large part of its recruitment from Detroit itself.

A notable location in Detroit is Croghan Street Station, which is in the basement of the Second Baptist Church in the Greektown neighborhood. This stop is thought to have given refuge to more than 5,000 freedom seekers.

George DeBaptiste, born a free Black man, devised an ingenious escape method for freedom seekers passing through Detroit on their way to Canada. As a wealthy entrepreneur, he had money and used it to purchase an entire steamship. The steamer's captain was a white man, and they cleverly disguised the boat as a commercial ship so as not to attract attention. But the true use of this steamship is now known today: It was used to move enslaved people to freedom in Canada across the river right under the noses of slave catchers.

Black Life in Canada

It's estimated that 15,000 to 20,000 fugitive enslaved people escaped the United States over the border into Canada between 1850 and 1860 and settled in Ontario. In total, 30,000 to 40,000 Black people entered Canada seeking freedom during the years of slavery in the United States.

During the nineteenth century, life was not all happy and easy once freedom seekers crossed the border into Canada. They faced similar racism to that found in the United States. The struggles were familiar as they found themselves fighting for access to nice places to live, equal education for their children, and better-quality jobs with fair pay.

Some of the jobs successful Black men and women established for themselves in Ontario included running grocery stores, hat shops, boutiques, an ice company, pharmacies, horse stables, a saw company, and carpentry businesses. The first taxi service in Toronto was also established by a Black man.

Despite the advances made for equality, many Black men and women chose to return to the United States after the Civil War ended.

As the United States moved toward abolishing slavery and the long struggle for reconstruction and civil rights, those men and women who bravely escaped slavery and then went on to help their fellow brothers and sisters still trapped in the South served as an inspiration for many generations to come, giving hope to Black people as they continued to face discrimination and unequal rights.

Chapter 8: Influences on American Literature and Art

The most well-known African American literature from the nineteenth century has come in the form of escaped enslaved people who have written their own narratives, telling of their experiences during daring escapes and the struggles they endured at the hands of their enslavers.

It would be easy to look over the fact that many Black writers contributed far more than just narratives about slavery. Among the esteemed Black authors of the 1800s, we can find those who wrote beautiful poetry, short stories, and novels about a wide range of subjects, including religion, suffrage, and more.

Today, we know that a person's skin color has nothing to do with their intelligence. However, in the nineteenth century, the United States was a world where Black people were looked down upon for the color of their skin. These authors proved to the world that those with Black skin were equally as capable of learning and creating as their white counterparts. Their great works of literature were proof of extraordinary intelligence. This was inspirational to other Black men and women and proof for abolitionists and civil rights activists to use in their continual fight for Black people's rights.

In addition to literature, African Americans of the nineteenth century also contributed striking paintings, even reaching international fame despite all the obstacles they faced. Their successes are still relevant today and continue to be studied by historians, artists, and writers.

Paul Lawrence Dunbar

Paul Laurence Dunbar.
https://commons.wikimedia.org/wiki/File:Paul_Laurence_Dunbar_circa_1890.jpg

Paul Lawrence Dunbar was a Black poet who was born in Ohio. His parents were born as enslaved people in Kentucky. In 1893, at age twenty-one, he shared his poetry at the Chicago World's Fair. His recently published volume of poetry was called *Oak and Ivy*.

Dunbar was known for writing poetry in what was referred to at the time as "Negro dialect." Today it would likely be called AAVE, or African American Vernacular English. He also wrote poetry in standard American-style English, as well as four novels.

Dunbar was one of the most famous and influential Black poets to make his mark on nineteenth-century literature. His literary works are now well known and thought to be the best representations of life for the Black man at the turn of the twentieth century in the United States.

Frances Ellen Watkins Harper

MRS. FRANCES E. W. HARPER,

Frances Ellen Watkins Harper.
https://commons.wikimedia.org/wiki/File:Mrs._Frances_E.W._Harper_NYPL_1225579.jpg

Frances Ellen Watkins Harper was a poet, author of short stories, and teacher at a school for free African Americans in Wilberforce, Ohio.

She was born on September 24, 1825, in Baltimore, Maryland, to free Black parents. Her parents sadly passed away before she was three years old, and Harper found herself in the care of her aunt and uncle, Henrietta and William Watkins.

Her uncle was a strong abolitionist, which influenced Harper throughout her life. Her uncle established his own school called the Watkins Academy for Negro Youth, which Harper attended until she was thirteen years old. As she had aged out of school at that point, she took a job as a nursemaid and seamstress for a white family.

To Harper's great joy, the white family owned a bookstore. She spent every free moment with her nose in a book. When she was twenty-one years old, she wrote her first volume of poetry titled Forest Leaves.

While she was working as a teacher in Pennsylvania, her home state of Maryland passed a law saying that free Black people were no longer welcomed in the state. If she returned home, she would be taken into slavery. This led to a turning point in Harper's life. She went to stay with friends of her uncle, who were also abolitionists. They were Letitia and William Still. You may remember the name William Still from earlier in the book. He became known as the "father of the Underground Railroad" for his major contributions to the movement.

Harper began writing poetry for the abolitionist newspapers. "Eliza Harris" was her first poem published in both *The Liberator* and in the paper owned by Frederick Douglass. In addition to traveling across the United States as a lecturer, Harper left an enduring mark on nineteenth-century literature. At the time, few Black women could read and write, as it was illegal for all people held as slaves to learn. Of those who had gained literacy, publishing short stories and poems was very unusual.

Her short story published in *Anglo-African Magazine* in 1859 was titled "The Two Offers." It was a story about the education of women. This publication was very significant because it was the very first short story published by a Black woman in the United States.[31]

Harper continued writing and touring, giving lectures and sharing her thoughts on women's rights, temperance, and the Black woman's fight for equality. She died in 1911 in Philadelphia, Pennsylvania, having made many wonderful contributions to both the women's suffrage movement and nineteenth-century literature during her lifetime.

Henry Ossawa Tanner

Henry Ossawa Tanner.
https://commons.wikimedia.org/wiki/File:Portrait_of_Henry_Ossawa_Tanner.jpg

---

[31] Frances Ellen Watkins Harper | National Women's History Museum

Henry Ossawa Tanner lived from 1859 to 1937. He was born in Pennsylvania as a free Black man. He was an acclaimed painter and one of the few Black men of the time to reach international fame for his art.

Tanner didn't begin his art career until 1876 when he started practicing by painting scenes from the Philadelphia harbor. He also painted local landscapes and animals from the Philadelphia Zoo. He was lucky enough to become the sole African American of his time to study for two years at the famous Pennsylvania Academy of the Fine Arts under the acclaimed Thomas Eakins.

From there, Tanner tried his hand at success in Cincinnati and Atlanta, but he struggled to sell his artwork. A bishop from Cincinnati, Ohio, purchased Tanner's entire collection of paintings, which enabled Tanner to fund a trip to Paris. Once in Paris, he became a student at the Académie Julian.

At the Académie Julian, he refined his technique, learning how to manipulate light and shadow to increase the dramatic effect of lighting in his works. He began painting biblical scenes, for which he would later become famous.

When 1894 rolled around, Tanner had reached a golden achievement for anyone, let alone a Black man from America. His paintings were on exhibit at the Paris Salon, which happened yearly. At the 1896 exhibit, he won an honorable mention. His painting was titled *Daniel in the Lions' Den*. He had painted it in 1895. In 1897, his painting *The Resurrection of Lazarus* won a medal at the Paris Salon exhibition. This was an amazing honor for Tanner, and even better, the government of Paris purchased his painting.[32]

---

[32] "Henry Ossawa Tanner | African American Painter, Religious Artist | Britannica"

Phillis Wheatley

Phillis Wheatley.
https://commons.wikimedia.org/wiki/File:Women_of_distinction_-_Phillis_Wheatley.jpg

Phillis Wheatley lived from 1753 to 1784. She is best known as the first enslaved African American woman to publish a book of poetry.

Wheatley was born in Gambia, Africa. In 1761, she was captured and brought to America, where she began her life as an enslaved person in Boston. At this time, Massachusetts was not yet a free state.

Although it was unusual for the time, her enslavers gave her an education. She learned very quickly, and in no time at all, she could read Greek classics, the Bible, and British literature. Her enslavers helped her publish her first poem when she was a teenager, in 1767.

In 1773, she traveled to London along with her enslaver's son. There, she published her first book of poetry, titled *Poems on Various Subjects, Religious and Moral.*[33]

Her writing reflected her pride in her African heritage, as well as the Christian religion she had been taught once she arrived in the United States. Her works played a major role in the literature and politics of the time. Abolitionists shared her writings, as did enslavers. In a racist world

---

[33] Phillis Wheatley | National Women's History Museum

that viewed Black men and women as less intelligent than those with white skin, she was clear proof that a Black person could read, write, and create works of literature just as well as anyone else.

Charles T. Webber

The Underground Railroad by Charles T. Webber.
https://commons.wikimedia.org/wiki/File:The_Underground_Railroad_by_Charles_T._Webber,_1893.jpg

Charles T. Webber was a prominent member of the artist community in nineteenth-century Cincinnati, Ohio. He became famous for his painting titled *The Underground Railroad*.

The painting was exhibited at the 1893 World's Columbian Exposition in Chicago. It depicted his good friends, who were abolitionists in Cincinnati. They were Levi Coffin, Coffin's wife Catharine, and Hannah Haydock. In the painting, the abolitionists are working to help a Black family reach freedom, traveling through a snowy winter scene with some measure of chaos. We don't know for certain, but it's thought the painting's scene takes place at the farm of Levi Coffin.

Webber is also well known for his many portraits. His painting of the Underground Railroad brought attention to the continuing struggle for equal rights during the Reconstruction period and inspired Black men and women to continue sharing their stories and struggles with the world.

Chapter 9: The Role of Women

In the 1830s, many women began to involve themselves in the abolitionist movement, fighting to end slavery. As they were rallying for the freedom of Black people, white women began to realize that they didn't have the same rights as men. It was at this point the women's suffrage movement quietly began to form. Women began to demand equal political rights, social rights, and economic rights. Before 1848, women did not have the right to attend any college or university for a higher education.

As the Civil War came to an end, lives in the United States were changing. Black people found themselves freed from the bonds of slavery, and a new battle for equal rights had begun. Women found themselves caught in the middle of this battle. All across the United States, those who had been abolitionists shifted their efforts into the fight for women's suffrage, working to end the view of women as the weaker sex. This effort aligned almost directly with the continuing fight for Black Americans to have full citizenship and equal rights as the white man.

Women worked behind the scenes to fight for equal rights, as well as openly giving speeches and even protesting. Black women found themselves doubly discriminated against as both women and racial minorities. White-led suffrage events often discriminated against and excluded Black women, who were told to march at the back of parades, if they were included at all.

Through the turbulent time in American history between the 1830s, the Civil War, and the turn of the century, many women rose up to proudly fight for their rights both racially and as females.

Harriet Tubman

Harriet Tubman.
https://commons.wikimedia.org/wiki/File:Harriet-Tubman-248x300.jpg

One of the most well-known figures of the Underground Railroad is Harriet Tubman. She was born as an enslaved person in Dorchester County Maryland in 1822. Her name at birth was Araminta Ross, and her enslaved parents were named Ben and Rit. Harriet married John Tubman while still enslaved in 1844.

When Tubman's enslaver died in 1849, she made her escape to freedom because she heard she was going to be sold to another plantation. She was upset at the number of family and friends she left behind in slavery and made it her personal mission to help them reach freedom.

Tubman spoke candidly about her situation and her actions in 1868 after the Civil War had ended and there was no longer any danger to her life. She said, "There was no one to welcome me to the land of freedom. I was a stranger in a strange land; and my home, after all, was down in Maryland, because my father, my mother, my brothers, and sisters, and friends were there. But I was free, and they should be free."[34]

Harriet used the skills she had learned working outdoors as a laborer to instruct others on how to follow the natural signs that pointed north as they fled. Many myths surround Harriet Tubman, including secret communication codes and the songs she would sing. She never used anything like the quilt codes that are talked about in US history classes or seen in movies and children's books. Instead, she relied on her instincts. She traveled in the water and through the woods in the dark of night, and she relied on her trust in fellow free Black abolitionists and some white allies.

Harriet Tubman carried a pistol with her on her journeys back to Maryland for a few reasons. The most striking reason she kept it was to threaten weaker enslaved people who became afraid and tried to turn back. Going back would give away everyone in the escapee party, risking all their lives. Harriet knew she couldn't allow that to happen.

Frederick Douglass said that, aside from John Brown, Tubman was the only person he had ever met willing to endure so many hardships to help her enslaved people.

Many people believe Harriet Tubman traveled all over the Southern United States to bring people to safety in the North. This is actually quite far from the truth. Tubman only returned to her hometown of Maryland about thirteen times to lead her family and friends north.

In total, Harriet Tubman brought seventy people northward from the Maryland area to freedom over the state lines. Though she had a bounty out with a cash reward for her capture, she was never given up or caught.

One popular Harriet Tubman myth is that she had a $40,000 bounty. However, the only evidence we have is of a $100 cash reward for the return of Harriet "Minty" Ross and her brothers. To put in perspective how ridiculous it would be for Tubman to have a $40,000 bounty on her head, consider that John Wilkes Booth, who shot Abraham Lincoln, had a bounty of $50,000. That's the equivalent of several million dollars today. If Tubman had a bounty that large, every newspaper across the North and South would have been advertising the reward, and she would surely have been captured.

---

[34] Bradford, Sarah H. *Scenes in the Life of Harriet Tubman*, 1868

Harriet Tubman became very well-connected in the North. She was friends with many well-known abolitionists and intellectuals of her day, including William Lloyd Garrison, Harriet Beecher Stowe, Ralph Waldo Emerson, and Bronson Alcott. (It was William Lloyd Garrison who gave Tubman one of her most famous nicknames: Moses, after the prophet in the Bible who led the Jews out of slavery in Egypt.) She befriended Frederick Douglass and also joined the suffragist movement, spending time with Lucretia Coffin Mott, Martha Coffin Wright, and Susan B. Anthony.

Word of her bravery and travels also spread across the ocean to England, where she was praised for her efforts.

During the Civil War, Tubman never backed down. She jumped in to continue helping, serving as a nurse for wounded African American soldiers in South Carolina. During that time, she was recruited by Major General David Hunter to be a spy for the Union behind Confederate lines. She helped guide three Union steamboats safely around Confederate mines.

On June 1, 1863, Tubman joined the 2nd South Carolina Infantry Regiment, led by Colonel James Montgomery. The infantry raided plantations along the Combahee River, where they rescued enslaved people and added them to their army. In total, the raids gathered more than 700 people. This was a significant raid that weakened the Confederate Army.

After the Civil War ended, Tubman threw all her energy into the women's rights movement for the last years of her life. She passed away at her home in Auburn, New York, in 1913.

What inspired Harriet Tubman to be so brave and determined? When asked, she said it was her unwavering Christian faith. During Tubman's younger years, the Second Great Awakening was happening. This was a Christian religious revival during which preachers traveled around the United States, sharing evangelical Christianity with both white and enslaved people on plantations across the South. These Christians believed it was their duty to share the message of the gospel to bring about a major reformation in the United States. This reformation would bring about the second coming of Jesus Christ, according to their beliefs.

Jarena Lee was one of the earliest female preachers to speak at the African Methodist Episcopal Church's revivals. Harriet Tubman said she drew inspiration from Jarena Lee. The realization that women could hold religious authority seemed to give Tubman power and resolve in her own life.

Tubman's beliefs were not purely evangelical Christian. Like many enslaved people from her time, she also held traditional African beliefs that had been fused with Christianity. We know this because an escapee that Tubman led to freedom talked about the charm she had given him to keep him safe.

A sudden injury to the head when Tubman was a teenager had almost taken her life. She was in a general store when slave catchers rushed in, trying to grab an escaped enslaved person. The insane slave catcher launched a two-pound weight at the man but instead hit Harriet Tubman, crushing part of her skull. After miraculously surviving this injury, Harriet would often get sudden painful headaches and fall asleep without warning, entering a trance-like state. She believed these trances were communications with God, and this is what made her fearless.

At only five feet tall, with or without trances from God, the tiny Harriet Tubman was a force to reckon with.

Sojourner Truth

Sojourner Truth.
https://commons.wikimedia.org/wiki/File:SojournerTruth.jpg

Sojourner Truth was born as Isabella Baumfree around the year 1797 in Swartekill, New York. She was an enslaved person who spent the first part of her life being bought and sold four times. In 1827, reckless bravery filled Sojourner Truth. She gathered her infant daughter and escaped. She made it to the home of a Quaker family named the Van Wageners, who purchased her freedom for $20.

While staying with the Quaker family, Sojourner had an intense religious experience that set the tone for the rest of her life. Sojourner Truth then began committing radical acts. The first thing she did was to ask the Van Wageners to help her sue the white enslaver who had purchased her enslaved child, who had been sold illegally. To the shock of many people, she won the case. She was the first Black woman to sue a white enslaver for custody of a child and win.

In 1843, she changed her name to Sojourner Truth. She believed God had called her to preach the truth, and she wanted her name to reflect that.

Sojourner made sexism as big of a part of her fight as racism. In 1844, she became a part of the Northampton Association of Education and Industry, which believed strongly in religious tolerance and pacifism.

She was inspired by Frederick Douglass to speak out about social justice, joining the fight to end slavery. Particularly, she focused on the rights of African American women and saw suffrage as interconnected with the issue of slavery. This belief set her apart from other outspoken abolitionists.

During one of her more famous speeches, Sojourner pointed out that, because she was a Black woman, no one stepped in to help her. If she wanted something to happen, she had to do it on her own. This was in response to male protestors at the women's convention where she had been giving her speech entitled "Ain't I A Woman?" She further put the sexist protestors in their place by pointing out that Christ was born from a virgin woman, meaning women had the power and resolve to do almost anything. Sojourner Truth was the only Black woman at this rally, but that didn't stop her from standing up for her rights and those of all the women present.

During the 1850s, Truth moved to Battle Creek, Michigan. This was where three of her daughters lived. From there, she helped enslaved people on their journeys to Canada. She also continued speaking across the United States about women's rights, Black equality, and temperance.

During the Civil War, she supported troops by organizing supplies. Once the war ended, Sojourner Truth was invited to the White House, where she then joined the Freedmen's Bureau. This organization helped newly freed enslaved people build skills and find new jobs to support themselves.

While in Washington, D.C. Sojourner spent her time lobbying against segregation. One day, a streetcar conductor thought he could violently stop her from catching a ride. He had no idea that he was messing with the wrong Black woman. Sojourner Truth had the man arrested and won her case against him in court.

She continued to fight for equal treatment of all Black people, regardless of whether they were male or female, until her death in 1883. In the last years of her life, she became almost completely blind and deaf. She returned to Battle Creek, Michigan, to be with her daughters in her final years.

Despite all her activism, Sojourner never learned how to read or write.[35]

Today, she is an inspiration for all Black feminists who find themselves caught in the intersectional space between racial rights and women's rights.

Lucretia Mott

Lucretia Coffin Mott lived from 1793 to 1880. She was a white woman who was born to Quaker parents in Nantucket, Massachusetts, as one of eight children.

Her parents sent her away to a Quaker boarding school in New York called Nine Partners. There, she heard stories from a Quaker abolitionist named Elias Hicks about the evils of slavery. Even at a young age, Mott was interested in social justice.

Once she learned that female teachers made less money than male teachers for doing the same job, she became enraged, and this began her path toward fighting for human equality.

In 1833, Mott worked with more than thirty other female abolitionists to create the Philadelphia Female Anti-Slavery Society. In 1840, Mott traveled to London, England, as a delegate from the society to attend the World Anti-Slavery Convention. While there, she met Elizabeth Cady Stanton, another abolitionist and champion for women's rights. The two ladies were furious when they found out that women were not allowed to

---

[35] Biography: Sojourner Truth

attend the World Anti-Slavery Convention.[36]

It would take eight years, but the pair went on to organize a women's rights convention in the United States to help educate men on this important topic.

Lucretia Mott stayed active for her entire life, participating in the women's rights movement and remaining an abolitionist, working for the equal rights of both women and Black people.

Elizabeth Van Lew

The men who planned battle strategies and led troops during the Civil War never imagined the role that shrewd, observant, and intelligent women might play in the conflict. Northern and Southern women alike immediately began gathering intel on their enemy. They observed the movement of troops, analyzed the enemy's strategies, and generally stood silently on the sidelines cataloging all kinds of important information without even being asked.

As soon as the generals and soldiers realized the uses they had for nosey women, they began to recruit them as undercover agents. These women were willing to risk their lives to help their army win the war.

Elizabeth Van Lew was forty-three years old at the start of the Civil War. She was a member of the elite rich community in Richmond, Virginia. This was the capital of the Confederacy, so Elizabeth was living in the heart of everything in a three-story mansion.

Though few realized it, Van Lew hated the institution of slavery. She wrote her thoughts in a secret diary that she kept buried in her backyard for safekeeping. She only revealed the location when she was on her deathbed.

Pretending to be a loyal Confederate throughout the entire war, Van Lew quietly offered her assistance to the Union. She spent the four years gathering and sending intelligence to important Union officers. Van Lew gathered and commanded her own network of spies for the Union Army. She did such an amazing job that she is now considered the most successful Union spy of the entire war.

When Libby Prison was used to house Union prisoners of war, Van Lew saw that the conditions were atrocious. She persuaded the general to allow her and her mother to bring food and medicine to the

---

[36] Lucretia Mott - Women's Rights National Historical Park (U.S. National Park Service)

imprisoned troops. The social elite of Richmond were horrified, and the mother and daughter were openly criticized for their work.

The *Richmond Enquirer* wrote, "Two ladies, a mother and a daughter, living on Church Hill, have lately attracted public notice by their assiduous attentions to the Yankee prisoners.... these two women have been expending their opulent means in aiding and giving comfort to the miscreants who have invaded our sacred soil."[37]

Shortly after, the mother and daughter experienced death threats from men all over the region. Van Lew doubled down her efforts, using a custard dish with a hidden compartment to pass messages to prisoners as she fed them. She concealed messages in books and then bribed guards to transfer prisoners to hospitals where they could be interviewed. At times, she hid prisoners in her home, assisting them in escaping. Few people suspected these two women would be intelligent or brave enough to carry out spy missions in this manner.

One escaped prisoner went back to the Union and reported the help he had received from Van Lew. This led to her official recruitment as a spy for the Union. She became the head of General Benjamin Butler's spy network. Her letters were written in a code, using colorless ink that only turned black when milk was poured on it.

In 1864, Van Lew had twelve people in her spying network, including her own Black servant, Mary Ann Bowser. They all worked together to pass clandestine messages filled with information between five locations.

By the end of the war, Van Lew had lost all her social standing in Richmond, and most of her money as well. She ended up living off donations from the families of prominent Union soldiers she had assisted during the war, dying alone as an outcast in her home in 1900.

Mary Ann Shad Cary

Mary Ann Shadd Cary was born in 1823 in Delaware, a slave state. Luckily, her parents were free African Americans, so Mary Ann wasn't born as an enslaved person despite living in Delaware.

When she was ten years old, her family moved to Pennsylvania, which was a free state and offered better opportunities for Mary Ann. She went to school in Pennsylvania, where she became a teacher. While

---

[37] Lineberry Cate: "Elizabeth Van Lew: An Unlikely Union Spy | History | Smithsonian Magazine"

living in Pennsylvania, the Shad family assisted fugitive Black men and women along the Underground Railroad.

After the Fugitive Slave Act of 1850, Mary Ann decided to go further north to Canada. It was there she met her husband, Thomas J. Cary. They had two children, and Mary Ann opened a school that served both Black and white students. Mary Ann Shad Cary made a name for herself when she became the first Black female newspaper editor in North American history. She published Canada's very first anti-slavery newspaper called *The Provincial Freedom*.

Mary Ann's husband died in Canada, and she decided to return to the United States just as the Civil War broke out. In Washington, D.C., she found employment as a teacher, writer, and political activist. She founded the Colored Women's Progressive Franchise Association.

Mary Ann spoke at the 1878 National Woman Suffrage Association Convention. She spent the rest of her life in Washington, D.C., fighting for equal rights for all people, regardless of race or gender. She died of stomach cancer in 1893, leaving behind a legacy to inspire women everywhere.

Chapter 10: The Legacy of the Underground Railroad

The Underground Railroad has left an everlasting legacy as part of the history of the United States of America, proving how people can unite to fight oppression.

That legacy bears witness to the barbaric acts the institution of slavery brought to America. Though we've tried to tone down and sometimes even hide the sordid truths about slavery, the pain and division remain a problem across the country as Black citizens continue to struggle for equal treatment and fight for healing.

The legacy of the Underground Railroad also leaves behind a story of freedom brought to enslaved men and women by extreme acts of bravery. In some instances, the bravery was their own sheer will and determination. In other instances, the bravery came from outside people, both white and Black abolitionists and free Black people living in the North.

Today, we are left with many historical sites that honor the memories of the brave people who came together to fight for equality and justice. There are also numerous museums dedicated to the legacy of the Underground Railroad all around the United States.

Harriet Tubman has a museum in her honor, the Harriet Tubman Underground Railroad Visitor Center located in Church Creek, Maryland, near the area where she lived. The museum has educational information and interactive exhibits, but the most powerful thing the museum offers is a thirty-six-site driving tour. This tour is self-guided and takes visitors to multiple locations along the Underground Railroad to see firsthand where people fled, hid, and cooperated on their path to freedom.

Cincinnati, Ohio, is home to the National Underground Railroad Freedom Center. This amazing museum honors the legacy of the Underground Railroad by offering lectures from current experts, information on how slavery still exists today and what we can do to fight it, educational short films, and extensive interactive exhibits. It's located along the Ohio River, the dangerous body of water many enslaved people risked their lives to cross to reach the free states in the North.

Slave Haven Underground Railroad Museum in Memphis, Tennessee, is another excellent site to explore the enduring history of the Underground Railroad. At this site, visitors can walk through a preserved antebellum home that was a stop along the Underground Railroad, including hidden trap doors and underground cellars where people hid. Open since 1997, the museum not only takes visitors back in time to experience the Underground Railroad in person but also bears witness to the long civil rights history in Memphis.

In Detroit, the memory of the Underground Railroad is alive and well. At the Underground Railroad Living Museum, visitors can experience live storytelling and become part of the story. Visitors are shackled in "Africa" and taken through an interactive experience, physically feeling the journey people took on their way to Detroit and then on to Canada.

In the United States today, the government has sponsored an excellent education initiative to promote factual information about the Underground Railroad's many contributors. This information is hosted on the National Park Foundation website, where in-depth biographies free of myths can be found. The initiative also extends to every level of the National Park System, partnering with state and local historical societies to include many locations across the US in the program. National Park-based educational programs include shows that reach young children, like the puppet show about the Underground Railroad given at a National Historic Site in Boston.

In 1998, legislation was passed to support this movement. It was called the National Underground Railroad Network to Freedom Act of 1998. The website states, "Through its mission, the Network to Freedom helps to advance the idea that all human beings embrace the right to self-determination and freedom from oppression."[38]

---

[38] "National Underground Railroad Network to Freedom".

Conclusion

Have you ever stopped to think what life in the United States would be like today if the Underground Railroad had never come into existence? Without encouragement and information from abolitionists and free Black people in the North, it's unlikely very many people would have had the knowledge or courage to escape their enslavers and head northward.

If you remember, it was the sheer number of Black men and women arriving in the Northern cities that brought issues between the North and the South to a head. This problem of whether Southern enslavers would be allowed to cross into the North to reclaim the escaped humans they viewed as their property was a catalyst for the Fugitive Slave Act of 1850, which ultimately led to the Civil War.

Without this catalyst, would we ever have had a Civil War? Or would things have remained stagnant, with African Americans enslaved in the South, and though free in the Northern states, still experiencing life with less than equal rights?

It's a sobering thought.

Without the enduring bravery of the men and women who worked to educate, embolden, and assist runaway enslaved people it's very likely our country would be in a completely different place right now.

When considering the Underground Railroad, remember it's far more than just a network of safe routes and abolitionists. The Underground Railroad represents something extremely significant.

The Underground Railroad was the United States' greatest movement displaying mass civil disobedience. Think about the gravity of thousands upon thousands of citizens, both Black and white, enslaved and free, coming together to subvert the United States government. This was an interracial political movement like nothing that had ever been seen before. People realized they needed to stand up for their neighbor's rights, and even in the face of breaking federal law, they still did it.

If we take away one important thing from the legacy of the Underground Railroad it should be that every person has the power to make a difference in this world by doing the right thing, even if it's done quietly and without recognition. Together, we have the power to make our country a better place for all people, equally.

If you enjoyed this book, a review on Amazon would be greatly appreciated because it would mean a lot to hear from you.

To leave a review:
1. Open your camera app.
2. Point your mobile device at the QR code.
3. The review page will appear in your web browser.

Thanks for your support!

Here's another book by Enthralling History that you might like

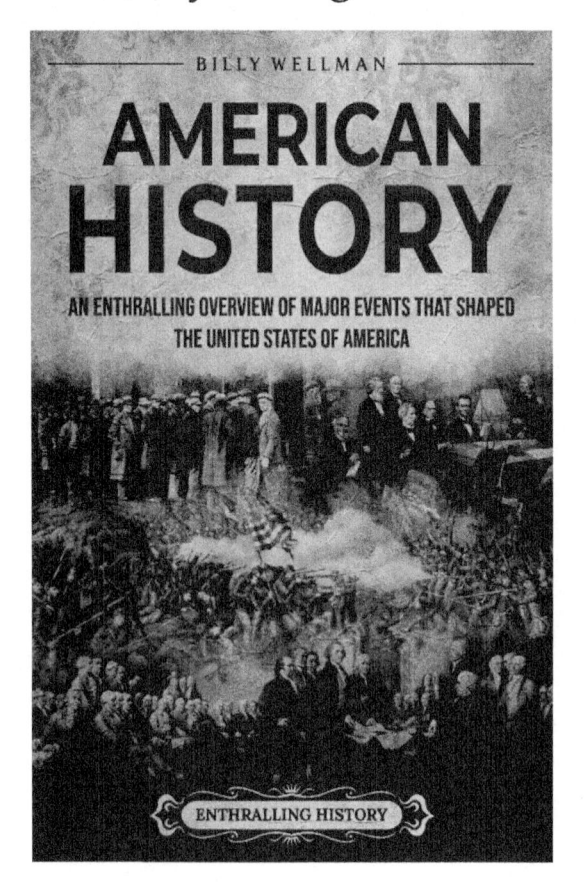

Free limited time bonus

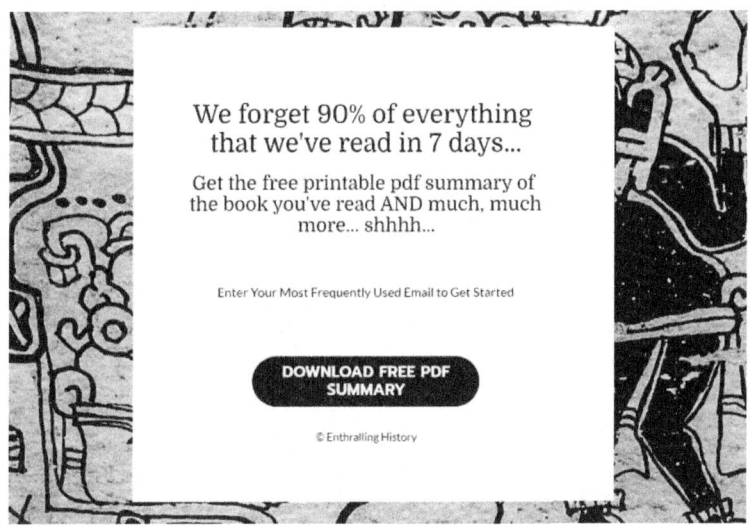

We forget 90% of everything that we've read in 7 days...

Get the free printable pdf summary of the book you've read AND much, much more... shhhh...

Enter Your Most Frequently Used Email to Get Started

DOWNLOAD FREE PDF SUMMARY

© Enthralling History

Stop for a moment. We have a free bonus set up for you. The problem is this: we forget 90% of everything that we read after 7 days. Crazy fact, right? Here's the solution: we've created a printable, 1-page pdf summary for this book that you're reading now. All you have to do to get your free pdf summary is to go to the following website: https://livetolearn.lpages.co/enthrallinghistory/

Or, Scan the QR code!

Once you do, it will be intuitive. Enjoy, and thank you!

Bibliography

1873 House Bill 0122. Resolve Providing For An Amendment Of The Constitution To Secure The Elective Franchise And The Right To Hold Office To Women, Massachusetts State Library, https://archives.lib.state.ma.us/handle/2452/742347; "Lewis Hayden Obituary," *The Woman's Journal* (Apr 13, 1889), Schlesinger Library, Radcliffe Institute, Harvard University, https://iiif.lib.harvard.edu/manifests/view/drs:49020444$123i.

"Abolitionist Movement - Definition & Famous Abolitionists | HISTORY"

"A Tour Of The Underground Railroad - Georgia Tourism Board"

"Back-to-Africa movement."

Bradford, Sarah H. *Scenes in the Life of Harriet Tubman*, 1868.

Brown Box, Henry *Narrative of the Life of Henry Box Brown, Written by Himself.*

"Dahomey," *The Liberator* (Boston, Massachusetts), February 20, 1863, Genealogybank.

Densmore, Christopher, "Quakers and the Underground Railroad: Myths and Realities"

Douglass, Frederick :*Narrative of the Life of Frederick Douglass.*

"Ellen Smith Craft | Georgia Women of Achievement."

"Frances Ellen Watkins Harper | National Women's History Museum"

"Frederick Douglass - History.com"

"Frederick Douglass PBS Biography"

Foner, Philip S., editor Taylor, Yuval *Frederick Douglass, Frederick Douglass: Selected Speeches and Writings*, editor. (Chicago: Lawrence Hill Books, 1975),180.

Gates Jr, Louis Henry "Myths About the Underground Railroad | African American History Blog | The African Americans: Many Rivers to Cross"

"Henry Ossawa Tanner | African American Painter, Religious Artist | Britannica"

Jacobs, Harriet A. *Incidents in the Life of a Slave Girl. Written by Herself: Electronic Edition*

"Josiah Henson (U.S. National Park Service)"

Kidder, Adams, Weems, *History of the Boston Massacre, March 5, 1770 : consisting of the narrative of the town, the trial of the soldiers and a historical introduction, containing unpublished* (Albany: J. Munsell, 1870), 255.

Lewis, Danny : "The New York Slave Revolt of 1712 Was a Bloody Prelude to Decades of Hardship | Smart News| Smithsonian Magazine."

"Lewis and Harriet Hayden House - Boston African American National Historic Site (U.S. National Park Service)"

Lineberry Cate : "Elizabeth Van Lew: An Unlikely Union Spy | History| Smithsonian Magazine"

Lucretia Mott - Women's Rights National Historical Park (U.S. National Park Service)

National Underground Railroad Network to Freedom

"Opinion | History's Tangled Threads - The New York Times"

"Opinion | How the Underground Railroad Got Its Name: - The New York Times

Phillis Wheatley | National Women's History Museum

Shane, Scott *Flee North: A Forgotten Hero and the Fight for Freedom in Slavery's Borderland.*

"To the Friends of the Fugitive," *The Liberator*, October 18, 1850.

The Liberator, December 29, 1865.

"Underground Railroad Secret Codes: Harriet Tubman"

"Underground Railroad." Quakers in the world.

"University Of Rochester Frederick Douglass Project"

"Weeksville - NYC's Early African American Settlements - Research Guides at New York Public Library Research Centers"

"Wilbur Siebert Historian or Fabulist | World History"

"William Still: An African American Abolitionist"

William Craft (U.S. National Park Service)
Women's History.org "Biography: Sojourner Truth"

Printed in Great Britain
by Amazon